I0571743

Advanced praise for *Smarter Together* and why you'll find it:

VALUABLE IN ANY INDUSTRY

"What *Smarter Together* proves is just how valuable sharing data can be when the terms of the exchange are clear, and the entire community's best interests are placed front and center. We need to use technology like Community Intelligence to make our world a better place, and Rob, as well as his company, Coupa, shows just how we can do so."

—GEOFFREY MOORE, Author of *Crossing the Chasm*

"Most books about the future are largely speculative. Rob Bernshteyn prefers to ask, 'What does the data say?' In a lucid, empirical account of how digital connection is changing the ground rules for business success, he explores the power of community in the digital era to make all of us smarter together on an industrial scale."

—PHIL WAINEWRIGHT, Co-Founder, Diginomica

"The impact digital transformation has had over the past decade can't be overstated; from redefining the way we travel, communicate, and do business, to drastically improving our ability to solve complex problems, data and digital are reshaping our world. In *Smarter Together*, Rob Bernshteyn anticipates the next evolution of this trend, where data from communities of users can provide collective intelligence, insights, and collaboration at a scale that's unprecedented. Digitally unlocking the long-standing power of communities has the potential to help solve some of the most long-standing and complex challenges we face in business and society today."

—MICKEY NORTH RIZZA, VP, Enterprise Applications and Digital Commerce Research, IDC

"At its core, business is a team sport. No one can win at business alone. It's important to keep that in mind as we face new challenges and disruptions in the marketplace. In *Smarter Together*, Rob Bernshteyn makes a fantastic case for how new technologies are helping individuals, companies, and even entire industries work together as a genuine community, for everyone's benefit. Building thriving communities around our organizations is the only way we can keep them healthy and growing for the long term. The community revolution that Rob describes and advocates for in *Smarter Together* is nothing short of a home run."

—JASON E. PEARL, Senior Vice President, Partnerships and Business Development, San Francisco Giants

VALUABLE TO YOUR COMPANY

"Rob and I share a deep belief, that 'none of us is as smart as all of us.' A diverse, transparent community that inspires one another is the modern foundation of building a successful business. In *Smarter Together*, Rob brilliantly showcases how Community Intelligence can revolutionize every industry and bring benefits to every individual looking to make a meaningful impact."

—JOHN FOLEY, Founder and CEO, Peloton

"In the past two decades, the most powerful consumer companies building the best products and business models have leveraged Community Intelligence in new ways to deliver tremendous value to users, to partners, and to investors. Google Search and Amazon Ratings are two examples that have morphed into trillion dollar companies by leveraging user data, implied or contributed, in creative ways, as have many others. These companies have taken on incumbents and seem to have a 'secret weapon' that incumbents do not have. That secret weapon can usually be mapped back to Community Intelligence. In the near future, most enterprise companies will either adopt this weapon or be destroyed by new entrants to their fields who do. Rob Bernshteyn's book is a great analysis of this weapon and a practical guide to how to use it in the business, rather than consumer, market. Your current or future competitor is reading it and applying it to your industry. Ignore it at your own peril."

—NOAM BARDIN, CEO, Waze

"Big data is no longer enough. The new battleground for business is agility and automation. Right now, there's a major shift happening—business applications are trying to solve more impactful challenges and it turns out those problems are incredibly difficult. Rob Bernshteyn, in *Smarter Together*, correctly calls out the need for innovative ways to use data to benefit not just a few savvy superusers, but everyone who touches and contributes to data sets. The idea of harnessing community data to offer greater intelligence, insight, and cooperative capabilities is a smart one, and something that many businesses should consider for themselves."

—MATTHEW BAIRD, Co-Founder and CTO, AtScale

"*Smarter Together* explores the benefits that business software promoting Community Intelligence is able to provide, including a worldwide collection of digital information that allows for increased agility for individual businesses, effective benchmarks for growth, and actionable insights into specific business practices. The combined experiences of individuals, once gathered into one shared collective, will give humanity an edge over machines in this rapidly evolving technological world. This is how humans will continue to thrive: together."

—CARLOS MOREIRA, Founder and CEO, WISekey,
Co-Author of *The transHuman Code*

VALUABLE TO YOU

"In my entire career, I've never met a more innovative, creative, and integrous thought leader than Rob. This book brings his iconic teachings to life, so the reader emerges being able to live up to their happiest and highest potential."

—SUZE ORMAN, The World's Personal Finance Expert

"What if software could share the brilliance of human endeavors, not automate us into oblivion? *Smarter Together* is a pioneering book about the power of human intelligence when we work together. A critical read for business leaders, and for the next generation as they grow their careers."

—GORDON RITTER, Emergence Capital

"Succinct and timely, Rob Bernshteyn's book *Smarter Together* underscores the need for collaborative thinking, evidence-based choices, and the right interplay between efficiency and respect for individuals. In a word, he's talking about balance, and why the best businesses know how to find it. A valuable read for seasoned decision-makers and first-time entrepreneurs alike."

–JAMES J. WARD, Privacy Lawyer and Data Strategist,
Co-Author of *Data Leverage: Unlocking the
Surprising Growth Potential of Data Partnerships*

SMARTER
TOGETHER

HOW COMMUNITIES ARE SHAPING THE
NEXT REVOLUTION IN BUSINESS

ROB BERNSHTEYN

AUTHOR OF *VALUE AS A SERVICE*

GREENLEAF
BOOK GROUP PRESS

Published by Greenleaf Book Group Press
Austin, Texas
www.gbgpress.com

Distributed by Greenleaf Book Group

For ordering information or special discounts for bulk purchases, please contact Greenleaf Book Group at PO Box 91869, Austin, TX 78709, 512.891.6100.

Design and composition by Greenleaf Book Group
Cover design by Greenleaf Book Group

Publisher's Cataloging-in-Publication data is available.

Print ISBN: 978-1-62634-706-9

eBook ISBN: 978-1-62634-707-6

Part of the Tree Neutral® program, which offsets the number of trees consumed in the production and printing of this book by taking proactive steps, such as planting trees in direct proportion to the number of trees used: www.treeneutral.com

Printed in the United States of America on acid-free paper

20 21 22 23 24 25   10 9 8 7 6 5 4 3 2 1

First Edition

To Kira, Tyler, Kyle, and Hailey

None of us is as smart as all of us.

—*Community Intelligence in 10 words*

CONTENTS

SECTION I

The Big Picture:
The Revolution in Context

EXECUTIVE SUMMARY

We will soon be able to draw upon the intelligence of the community, in real time, to benefit the community, our companies, and ourselves—transforming entire industries in the process. Commerce will never be the same again.

For example, we will know—

- The best ways to leverage communities to dynamically collaborate and gain an advantage over those outside the community

- Real-time best practices for virtually every element of our business that we can enact instantly to maintain optimal business performance

- The best options at any given moment for any specific product or service we might desire or that our company needs

- Who delivers exactly what they say they will, on time, with the best price, best practices, and with the quality we desire—and which suppliers are risky and which have the highest likelihood of running out of inventory or even going out of business

- And this is just the beginning . . .

How can we make everything I just talked about and more happen? Let's start with the simple concept of aggregating community data anonymously for the benefit of the community itself. There is already a prototype for the way this works. And I bet you're already familiar with it.

BABY, YOU CAN DRIVE MY CAR

If you have ever used Waze, the community-based traffic and navigation app, you know how effective it is. There is a reason more than 100 million people worldwide are using it—and just how huge of a breakthrough it was.

It wasn't all that long ago, if you were driving someplace unfamiliar, you'd get a road map. The first one was created 115 years ago, and things improved—albeit slowly—from there.

In the 1930s, the American Automobile Association (AAA) created TripTik. You could call AAA—or send them a letter (people used to do that, honest)—and ask them to create a detailed route that could get you from point A to point B, say from Albany, New York, where I went to undergraduate school, to San Mateo, California, where I work today. AAA would create a personalized map for you, which was actually a number of highlighted maps presented in booklet form.

Flash forward a bit. By the 1990s you could get directions online from MapQuest. Freestanding navigation devices like Garmin and

TomTom followed, and it then became possible to create maps in your smartphone that provided turn-by-turn directions.

But Waze goes dramatically beyond that. As you drive with the Waze app open on your phone, you are sharing *passively* (meaning you don't have to do a thing) real-time information that is sent to the company and comes back to you in the form of real-time traffic conditions, which allows the app to suggest route options—also in real time. So the driving community, including you and me on the road, is actually creating information that is helping the community get where we're going faster.

As the company, now owned by Google, explains: "The maps and navigation are powered by users. The more people drive with Waze open [Waze is pinging your cell phone once a second, measuring your speed and the route you are taking], the better the navigation."

In other words, the community, which for Waze is now 115 million strong, is creating the best way to get from points A to B at any given time.

As Waze puts it: "By connecting drivers to one another, we help people create local driving communities that work together to improve the quality of everyone's daily driving. That might mean helping them avoid the frustration of sitting in traffic, cluing them in to a police trap, or shaving five minutes off of their regular commute by showing them new routes they never even knew about."

(In addition, you can also use the app to report accidents, speed traps, potholes, and the like. That information also is instantly shared with other users.)

So, you understand why I like comparing the coming Revolution in business to what Waze is already doing for drivers.

Waze is all about contributing to the *common good* out there on the road. I envision us coming together to create the common good for all of us when it comes to running our businesses and doing our jobs better. As with Waze, we will be smarter together.

FACTS, NOT OPINIONS

There are a couple of great things about getting information about the community from the community.

The first is that you are truly getting behavior-based data and not opinions. People are not saying, "I *think* Supplier X's prices are too high." They are saying, "We are *seeing* from the data that Supplier X's prices are consistently 8 percent to 10 percent more than his competitors."

The second great thing is that you are getting information from every member of the community. That is *not* what typically happens. Think about the reviews you read on Yelp or Amazon.

When reviewing a restaurant, for example, often only the "madvocates" (people who didn't like their experience) and maybe a few advocates will bother to write something. But everyone else—and that everyone else is probably the majority—is silent. So, you are only getting the two extremes. That's not truly showing us intelligent information based on everyone's behavior. Much data is missing from both indifferent and content customers. That is no way to get an accurate picture.

In addition, these reviews capture only a small fraction of the data—you might learn from reading a review that a restaurant is known for making a wonderful chicken dish, but you don't hear about the other 19 entrees they offer.

That lack of complete information could make the dining experience less than it could be. (Wouldn't you like to know how good the rest of its offerings are? You might not eat chicken.)

WHY IS THIS POSSIBLE NOW?

Why hasn't the Revolution I am calling for happened before? Because it wasn't possible before, but now it is. There are three reasons why.

First, we finally have the technology that makes it possible to collect and aggregate mass amounts of data nonintrusively.

Second, the horsepower to crunch these massive data sets (and the more information we have, the more accurate the findings can be) is finally available, and so are the algorithms necessary to sort the data to provide meaningful interpretations for a community hungry to get valuable real-time insights.

And third, we are entering into a business environment where there is increased willingness among people and companies to share information, in an anonymous fashion, and collaborate.

That's a big change. There used to be a mindset—and you can still find it in some "old school" executives—that hoarding information gives you power. And so they would hoard it. That was the way you got promoted: knowing things that other people didn't.

The business environment has changed since then. People now understand it is extremely difficult to hoard information. Nearly everything is available online if you search long enough. And more and more of us have grown up in a world where connecting is taken as a given, because we have seen the benefit. Think LinkedIn, Twitter, other forms of social media, and the like. What can flow out of a connection is collaboration, enabled by technology, of course. And collaboration, in part, makes us a community.

> *Data/intelligence, information sharing,*
> *and collaboration make up the three key*
> *components of community power.*

Increased connection and collaboration are the new norm. That is why you are seeing more and more "frenemies," or fiercely competitive companies, deciding to collaborate with each other from time to time. Airlines that battle head-to-head in some markets have created alliances so that their passengers can get to cities they do not serve. Pharmaceutical companies that compete in one area—say, in their offerings for high blood pressure medication—will work together in another to enter a new field (e.g., cancer) in which they do not. And it happens all the time in high tech and entertainment. Amazon Prime and Netflix seemingly are engaged in a fight to the death in the battle for streaming videos, yet Netflix uses Amazon Web Services' cloud hosting for its service.

Given these examples, it is not a stretch to say that even the fiercest competitors who would not share any information about their strategy or marketing plans would be willing to share information such as spending data because it could benefit them ("Hey, look, that supplier we are using is not as good as the one we have never tried, according to the information shared by the community, the Community Intelligence"), transforming the entire industry in the process.

PRIVACY AND RECIPROCITY

If the Revolution I am calling for is to work, it requires two major components: privacy and reciprocity. Let's touch on both. (We will go into this in depth in Chapter 4).

Very few people are going to share what is otherwise proprietary information about how their companies are run (e.g., what they're spending and on what) if there is a risk that the information will be attached by name to either them or their company. **That's why anonymity is the key here.** Waze is only interested in where you—and all of us—are on the road at any given time so it can predict traffic slowdowns and jams. Who you are and what kind of vehicle you drive are irrelevant. These only become relevant if you desire to be known, and even then, you are often known as simply an anonymous Waze icon. It's the same when it comes to community collaboration. We might just want to know what you are spending on pencils and if they arrived on time, to offer a ridiculously basic example. We don't need to know who you are, and the only thing we need to know about your company is what business it is in—financial services, health care—so we can create apples-to-apples comparisons when we share the data.

One reason people have privacy concerns is that they are afraid their information is going to be sold. But in this Revolution, what happens to your information is explained transparently up front—you are contributing your data to get value in exchange (i.e., insights from the broader community); nothing more, nothing less.

The second point? Even if you are assured your information is never going to be attributed to you or sold, there needs to be a reciprocity component. It's human nature to want to feel you are at least getting as much in return as you are giving, and perhaps a bit more.

There are two ways that can happen. The first is if the information is provided with little or no effort on your part. Again, let's use Waze as an example. You literally don't have to do a thing to provide information—Waze just pings your phone. So you do nothing and get real-time traffic insights in return. It's a good deal. (Of course, you can report speed traps, potholes, and the like if you wish, but it isn't required for you to receive Waze's traffic information and step-by-step directions.)

The other way reciprocity happens is if you feel you are getting substantially more in return than you are giving. You allow access to transaction data (what your company bought, from whom, when, and what you paid in an anonymized way) and you get back something that is going to help your company, advance your career, and make you more valuable within your company.

What you are giving isn't much, but you are getting a lot back in return.

We have seen the power of community forever

You have probably heard the saying "All of us are smarter than any one of us" or some variation of it. (We used a variation for the epigraph of this book. It's almost become a cliché.)

But clichés often become clichés for a reason: They're true. This one is, and it always has been, going back to mankind's earliest days, when we lived in tribes. One person with a spear was good—they could hunt for food and defend themselves—but an entire tribe with spears was better when it came to defense and hunting efficiently.

The big premise here is that working together is better than working separately. That is as true today as it was when the first tribes formed.

Think of the elders of those tribes. They were respected, in part, because of their age, but more so because they were the source of wisdom. Where did that wisdom come from? It came from having a huge amount of data about how the world (in their case, the community) worked.

> Today, you don't have to live multigenerationally and receive information from some old guy's head. You can have it all in real time in front of you.

PLAYING OFFENSE AND DEFENSE AT THE SAME TIME

Used a pay phone lately? Dropped off any film to be processed? Bought a map? Ordered encyclopedias? Placed a classified ad? Sent a fax? Backed up your data on a floppy disk or CD-ROM? Rented a movie from a stand-alone video store like Blockbuster? Used a travel agent to book a routine vacation or business trip? Searched for something in the Yellow Pages?

Making a better buggy whip, a faster film camera, or a quieter typewriter won't keep the stagecoach operators, film processors, or typesetters employed.

Of course you haven't. All of those products and services were disrupted out of business—made obsolete by innovations that, in nearly every case, the established competitor didn't see coming or didn't fully understand the threat therein, if they did.

Having up-to-date information can help you—

- Keep from being blindsided by some emerging trend that is destined to upend your business model. You can bet that the folks who run the Yellow Pages wished they had paid more attention to the new-fangled thing called online advertising, which started to pop up (literally) in the 1990s. It is cute that the Yellow Pages is now branding itself as "the original search engine." But that simply underscores what a gigantic opportunity it missed.

- Solve the **Innovator's Dilemma**—by making sure you are not a victim of it in the first place.

In *The Innovator's Dilemma*, the late Harvard Business School professor Clayton Christensen showed how even great companies could do everything right and still lose their market-leading positions—or even fail—as new and often unexpected competitors entered and took over their markets.

The problem he described is *not* the result of bad management. Leaders of established, successful companies in nearly every case made the rational decision to focus on activities that addressed customers' needs, promised higher profits, were technologically feasible, and allowed them to compete in large markets.

But as Christensen pointed out, it is extremely difficult for a large, successful, established company to alter the way it does things. By the time a new entrant—such as online ads—is recognized as a threat, it is too late for an established company such as the Yellow Pages to respond effectively.

However, if you are getting updated information about your industry daily, it becomes dramatically easier to navigate and respond. For example, if you were in the print advertising business a couple of decades ago, you would have been able to see what percentage of overall advertising spending was going to online advertising and that the percentage was steadily climbing.

Seeing in real time what is going on gives you time to

experiment. Nothing would have prevented the Yellow Pages, for example, from offering its own version of online advertising early on. That would have kept them from being completely locked into print when the world decidedly was going the other way. Having established a position in online advertising, they could have shifted more and more resources to the online market as it grew. Instead of being blindsided by the new emerging business model (online advertising), they could have benefited from it (particularly given their established brand).

Innovator's Dilemma addressed.

WHY JOIN THE REVOLUTION

How does this big idea of sharing your information anonymously with the rest of the community help your company, you, and the community?

Let's take those categories one at a time.

WHAT'S IN IT FOR COMPANIES?

The most obvious advantage is **benchmarking**.

Companies are always trying to figure out how they stack up against—and beat—others. The problem is, as you know, that they are using rudimentary, outdated ways to figure that out. They do some surveys, collect some third-party data, and bring in some consultants. But the data is dated and not necessarily correct (not having access to all industry data can skew the results).

Also, it is extremely rare that the data generated by benchmarks allows a company to make real-time adjustments to help them compete. It's not as if you are running a cross-country race where you can see at a glance that there are three people in front of you and four behind, and you know at any given second where you stand. Organizations don't have any of that information in real time.

It doesn't have to be that way. If there were a willingness to share information anonymously, have it aggregated, and then have it delivered back, businesses could have information that was relevant, real time, and valuable. Then they would be able to course-correct in a much more agile way. They might get into new product lines more quickly. They might spend less time on certain internal processes. They might hire from different talent pools. All areas of the company could get better.

Beyond benchmarking, the ability to draw on what the community knows and is willing to share—Community Intelligence—fosters two key outcomes:

- **Faster decision-making.** If you are aware of best practices in your industry, you don't have to waste time figuring them out on your own. You can move faster. No small feat these days.

- **Increased operating efficiency.** That's the logical conclusion that flows from benchmarking and faster decision-making.

Nearly every part of running a business will become a bit easier for **leaders**. The benchmarking will identify best practices as well as useful metrics. Additionally, leaders will have a more rigorous framework for judging employee performance, since they will be able to compare their employees to workers at other organizations.

Without information, you can rationalize anything away. With information, you can avoid blind spots.

We can think about this information sharing in terms of new carrots and sticks. The carrot is the opportunity to be much better and win the market, which will lead to bonuses, getting paid more, and job security. The stick is that it forces you, the leader, to deal with reality head-on. You may have been thinking everything's fine, but you weren't comparing your company's performance to anything. If you had real-time, cross-company data, you'd know whether your company's decisions are great or not.

So, it is clear that Community Intelligence can be of huge importance to companies, but its impact goes beyond that. It can improve how employees do their jobs, and even transform entire industries.

All of this is possible even without getting into community collaboration and other community dynamics that can drive value.

WHAT'S IN THIS FOR YOU?

Employees will benefit in two ways:

- Having all of this information will allow you to do your job better. In real time, you will have access to industry-wide best practices so you know what works and what doesn't.

- You will know how you are performing vis-à-vis your peers, which will make it easier for you to make your case for a raise, a promotion, and the chance to make a greater impact.

WHAT'S IN IT FOR THE COMMUNITY IN GENERAL?

The advantages of the Revolution for customers, and buyers of all kinds, are obvious and numerous. As we run through these benefits quickly, you will see how entire industries could change:

- **Companies will compete harder for your business.** They will have a handle on what the industry standards are and know they will have to exceed them to get, and keep, your business.

- **You will be offered new products and new solutions to your problems faster.** Since companies will be closer to their customers, they will be able to move more quickly to respond to their (your) needs.

- **The service you receive will be faster and the products better**, since you will know which suppliers to use and which to avoid.

- **You will get better deals (Part I).** You will have a handle on what others are paying, which will help you avoid paying too much.

- **You will get better deals (Part II).** The increased competition will help keep prices down. Since your suppliers will be able to operate more efficiently, they should be able to pass along some of their savings.

- **You will get better deals (Part III).** You might be able to pool your purchases with others in the community who need the same goods, and get a deeper discount as a result.

- **It will be easier to find the right suppliers**—not only those who are the most reliable but also those, for example, who do ethical sourcing.

- **You will have better fraud protection and risk management.** Instead of having to react after the fact, you will have information ahead of time to alleviate risk, since the community will flag those who routinely overbill or who might go bankrupt.

Perhaps the easiest way to put it is that consumers—whether we are talking business-to-business or business-to-consumer—will have more control over the buying process.

WHAT'S AHEAD: HOW THE BOOK IS ORGANIZED

In Chapter 1, **Welcome to the Future**, we will provide the context for our belief that communities are shaping the next revolution in business. We are moving to a world where you have to sell a specific outcome, not a product or service, and drawing on what the community knows will allow you to do that efficiently.

Chapter 2 provides in detail the business case for using Community Intelligence. Specifically, we will discuss the advantages that come from using it, and we also will explain what could happen to your organization if you choose to go it alone.

From there we will look in detail at the three main components that compose the power of Community Intelligence: data/intelligence; information sharing; and collaboration and the pooling of power. We'll use the example of business spend management—how you can get a stranglehold on your costs—to demonstrate.

That discussion in Chapter 3 will underscore something you have already noticed—the three components of community power build on themselves. The first (data/intelligence) involves knowing what you want to do. The second (information sharing) is working with people to do it. And the third (collaboration and pooling of power) is leveraging what you have to work together and drive results.

From there, we will take head-on the subject I get the most questions about when I advocate for the sharing of information: privacy. And as you will see in Chapter 4, it is less of a concern than you may think.

You picked up this book, in large part, to determine how you can benefit from it. And that will be the subject of the following three chapters.

In Chapter 5, **What's in It for Your Company**, we will show the advantages that flow to your company from using Community Intelligence.

Companies don't do anything. Their people do. And part of the appeal of this book, we think, is that it points out how employees of a company using the power of community can personally benefit. That will be our focus in Chapter 6, **What's in It for Your Employees?** It will show them the best way of doing things—which suppliers they should use, how long things like processing invoices should take, and whether they deserve a raise. (They will have data that shows they are outperforming their peers at similar companies, saving their company substantial sums of money, etc.) Simply having dramatically more information will allow them to do their jobs better and increase their personal reputations.

The upshot of everything we will have talked about in the first six chapters can lead to only one conclusion: Exponential change is possible when all of the companies within an industry draw on community data. That means the industry has the potential to change for the better. That is what we will be talking about in Chapter 7, **How This Can Move an Industry.**

We end with two looks at the future sandwiched around a short summary, Chapter 9. The first, as we point out in Chapter 8, shows that the future (in part) is already here, and we highlight a number of organizations that are already putting Community Intelligence to work today. And in Chapter 10 we end with a fun look at what the future could look like, in the very near term.

As you will see, what is exciting and even more intriguing is that we have already started down that path.

Let's begin.

> **With global competition and digital transformation becoming even more pronounced, the pressure on companies to understand the value they offer, and to articulate that properly, will only grow. Community Intelligence can help. A lot.**

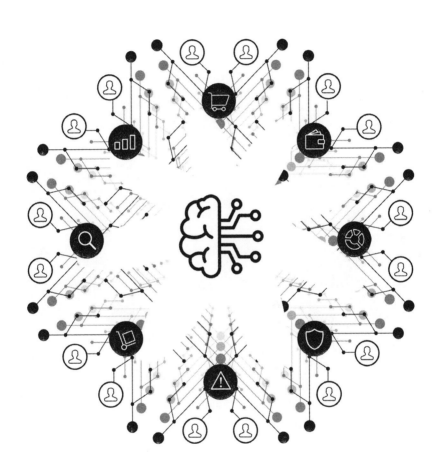

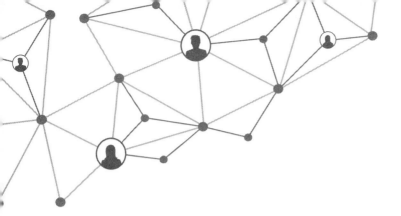

Chapter 1

WELCOME TO THE FUTURE

Let me begin with this chapter's main takeaway: Going forward, purely transactional relationships—that is, you buy something from someone and that is the end of the relationship—will occur less and less frequently. Subscriptions and results-based selling ("If you don't get the outcome/value we agreed on, you don't pay") will become the norm.

Why am I predicting this kind of future?

It is simply the logical conclusion of the way businesses have been evolving.

I think all companies will go through three phases, or waves, of commerce:

Wave 1. They simply offer a product or service.

Wave 2. They provide Value-as-a-Service. (I will explain what that is, if you are not familiar with the term.)

Wave 3. Companies will be able to offer exponential value thanks to Community Intelligence. (This is the wave we are about to enter.)

These three waves/phases could sound a little vague in the abstract, so let's get specific by showing how these trends could play out in the tech industry, by reprising an example from my own industry that I used in my previous book, *Value as a Service*.

Think back to the 1990s, when we were squarely in **Wave 1** (transactional relationships).

Enterprise software—which includes things like handling online payments or customer relationship management and is used to satisfy the needs of an organization rather than those of an individual user—had been a product-based world for decades. The product was first sold and deployed on mainframes and was later distributed through CDs (during the client-server era). But it was always a product. A company would make something physical, put it into a box, and ship it to a customer.

> *Purely transactional relationships are going away*
> *(and probably sooner than you think).*

In that first wave, you bought enterprise software from someone, and that could essentially have been the end of the relationship. The problem was that a significant portion of big deployments never delivered the anticipated value.

What we had was a one-sided relationship, in that all the risk rested with the customer. The customer paid up front; the software company shipped them the product, and then it was basically up to the customer to make it work. To add insult to injury, customers also had to wait to buy the next iteration to take advantage of any upgrades.

While that sounds like a great deal for the software providers, it really wasn't. For one thing, they had to deal with functions that were not part of their core competencies—even little things like producing the CDs and packaging and distributing them, for example. The business model also made for uneven revenue flow, which meant the providers scrambled every quarter to make their numbers, resulting in a stressful existence.

Yes, the company made money (sometimes a lot of it) selling the software and made a bit more by providing maintenance and technical support, but the business model didn't lead to great sustainable outcomes for anyone.

Enterprise software companies back then were in the production and transaction business: Produce the CD, sell the CD, and then either go out and find another customer or wait until it had an upgraded version to sell to its existing customers. They were strictly transaction oriented.

That's the way it was until we got to the second wave: Value-as-a-Service, which is where a lot of enterprise software companies are today.

Today, a software company can take their product, install it in a secure, remote virtual environment—whether at their headquarters or on a third-party platform—and have their clients access it directly. The way we consume software today is similar to how we consume electricity. There is a remote source that any single customer (or household) can subscribe to in order to receive value—the electricity—and they pay for what they use.

It is clear that software-as-a-service (SaaS) provides a much better value proposition and lower up-front risk to the customer. Before SaaS was an option, if you bought a $3 million product from a software company, you'd own that product and all of the risks that came with it, forever. It was your (the customer's) responsibility to get it to work the way you hoped it would. And whether it did or not, you were still out the $3 million.

With the subscription model, you're still likely to be paying the same $3 million, but it will be spread out over three years—a million dollars a year for a three-year subscription, as an example.

The advantages of the subscription model are obvious:

- You do not have to pay the entire $3 million at once.

- If the product does not perform as agreed, you may be able to cancel, saving the rest of the subscription price.

- It's quicker. You get up and running faster. There is less software to configure. You plug directly into the service.

- You don't have to wait until the next full iteration of the software is available to get upgrades; you can receive them as the vendor completes them and makes them accessible.

- On a related point, if the vendor is really good, they are incorporating, in real time, key suggestions from anyone who uses the software, so everyone can benefit almost immediately from the improvements.

You see why I describe the second wave as Value-as-a-Service. The very best SaaS vendors are well underway in moving to a Value-as-a-Service mindset and approach. They have moved from the transaction model in Wave 1 to the simple idea in Wave 2 of not only delivering their offerings in an "as-a-service" model, but also delivering results that will lead to quantifiable improvement: this much saved, this much improvement in lead generation, this much improvement in revenue, this much improvement in employee retention.

The relationship between buyer and seller increasingly works like this: You pay a fee, and in return we give you something of value that can be clearly and distinctly articulated.

I can't imagine going back to the old days of the purely transactional model with all of the risk on the buyer. In fact, I think we are now entering Wave 3. Why? With the second wave now firmly in place among leading companies, customers seek even more. That's always the way business works.

FROM HERE TO THERE

I ended my last book by saying that as the world becomes more and more competitive, companies will receive greater and greater pressure to deliver clear, quantifiable, value-based outcomes to their customers. By drawing on what the community knows—Community Intelligence—they're better suited to deliver that.

Why? Here are three quick examples:

1. Drawing on Community Intelligence could provide better benchmarks so that companies can improve in all areas—spending, recruiting, marketing, IT, and so on.

2. Companies could gain better insights into their suppliers (Part I). Who is giving the best deals? Can we consolidate our spending with fewer vendors to gain economies of scale?

3. Companies could gain better insights into their suppliers (Part II). An increasing number of customers will only do business with firms that are locally and ethically sourced or use sustainable materials. It will be easier to find suppliers who meet specific needs.

The net result is you will be able to deliver more value by being more thoughtful in planning your strategies based on Community Intelligence, as well as operationally more efficient in doing so. You will know you are doing business with suppliers who are offering the lowest prices. That can help you both boost your margins and allow you to offer lower prices. And you will also know that you have the best employees (based on industry benchmarks) who are performing optimally.

Every company will be better positioned to drive value through the use of Community Intelligence.

The upshot from the third wave of business? Commerce will be fully optimized. Consumers will get exactly what they want from the products or services they buy, and suppliers will get successful repeat customers.

This is extremely important because, again, providing value will be the battleground going forward. We won't be competing on products or services. We will be competing on the basis of how much value we can deliver to our customer. That is really what customers want and what they are buying. Not only will we be able to save them money—because our costs are lower and we are operating more efficiently—we will help them run their own businesses better, because we will be able to give them visibility into what is going on in their industry. (See Chapter 7.)

So the evolution of business looks like this. We go from simply offering a product (Wave 1) to providing Value-as-a-Service (Wave 2) to offering exponential value thanks to Community Intelligence (Wave 3). This is the way business is evolving, and quite frankly, we have no choice but to do business this way for three important reasons:

1. Some 90 percent of the world's data has been created in the last two years. Some 2.5 quintillion (2,500,000,000,000,000,000) bytes of data *daily* is now brought into existence, according to IBM, which says the rate is likely to accelerate.

2. The world is now definitely "flat," a shorthand way of saying fully connected. Advances in technology have made it possible to do business, or almost anything else, instantaneously with billions of other people across the planet. (We no longer think twice about using Skype or FaceTime to talk to someone literally halfway around the world. The fact that you likely think these are commonplace examples shows how far we have come.)

3. The world is moving faster than ever, and, to echo IBM's prediction, I can't imagine it slowing down anytime soon. Given the pace at which businesses are changing and the increased competition, commerce is moving too quickly for us to go it alone. And competition is not only becoming greater but also catching up to you faster, no matter how wonderful your product or service. You're competing with everyone in the world because the people in your industry can access your customers, and you can access theirs. The world has become a far smaller place.

Community Intelligence will give us an opportunity to deliver even more value to our customers in an increasingly hypercompetitive business environment.

In this smaller, faster-moving world, you need to draw on every resource you can. And Community Intelligence is certainly a major one.

WHERE THIS IDEA CAME FROM

I have been thinking about the idea of drawing on the knowledge of the community to benefit the community for almost 20 years. It started back when I was in graduate school, after a couple years of working in the tech industry.

I was in the MBA program at Harvard Business School (HBS). During the two years that I was working toward my degree, my mind was completely focused on how CEOs solve problems. My classmates and I read literally hundreds of business cases from every industry, we heard guest lectures from the CEOs themselves, and we would listen to our professors describing the trials that people who run organizations deal with.

Eventually, if you are paying attention, you're able to spot commonalities in those challenges, such as those involving leadership, strategy, execution, competitive differentiation, and complex competitive dynamics. Reading and thinking about and discussing all of those challenges allows you to develop pattern recognition. You see what all these business cases have in common.

Doing this work in business school is exhausting. You go to classes all day and read and highlight cases every night. You never really see the outside. So, one of the things I did during the summer between semesters was to buy a bike at a garage sale to force myself to go outside once in a while and get some exercise.

I rode it around Cambridge, Massachusetts, where the business school is located, and sometimes I would ride along the Charles River toward MIT, where I would see their artificial intelligence (AI) lab, which wasn't much back then. (I started business school in 2000.)

I had always been interested in AI, and I was convinced it would have a major impact on business. Pedaling around the AI lab got me to thinking about how we could use AI to solve the business challenges we were studying.

That was one genesis of my thinking about employing the power of community. Another was all of the people I saw as I rode around the campuses of my school and MIT. For the most part, everyone was working in a collegial environment. They were working together on tasks. That underscored for me the fact that, together, people were stronger and more effective than they were when they worked individually. It was a true community experience. It was living proof that even if we are talking about the brightest people, all of us are smarter than any one of us.

And that, by the way, was exactly how it worked in the classroom at HBS. With every one of the cases we looked at, we did not solve them individually—we worked in teams. Every person's viewpoint, when taken together, helped us make the smartest choices in how to take a business forward and solve the problem at hand. It was a group information-sharing process that informed each person's ultimate view on any particular subject.

So that was another piece that went into my thinking: How could you draw on the community and apply it to the industry I came from—technology?

The more I thought about it, the more I understood that putting AI and community together made sense. If you could get people to work together and share information, and then use technology to leverage their thinking, tasks could be a lot more efficient. It just made a lot of sense. It would be a way to bring business forward, especially my industry. (I was working in enterprise software back then.)

All I'd ever done was implement software. And, by the way, that implementation did not take into account the ideas we just discussed. It was not done thoughtfully. There was nothing collaborative about it, with the exception of what I carried in my head from one project to another. And definitively, there was no intelligence sharing. Every company kept their information strictly to themselves.

I kept thinking about the idea of leveraging the knowledge of the community through technology and collaboration. Why? Because I was in classrooms thinking about business and collaborating with my classmates. I could also see the changes coming about because of technology and AI—I even took a course at MIT to learn more—and I realized that all of these things could come together to make companies operate more efficiently.

Now at the time, the melding that I was imagining wasn't yet possible for a number of reasons:

- AI wasn't there yet.

- The computer power was lacking.

- The technology wasn't agile enough to mine massive data stores and share what was learned. It was all client-server topology back then. It took years to install, and you needed a PhD to modify it. It was simply too rudimentary to be able to support business needs at speed.

- You couldn't collaborate because there was no interplay between companies. Each company was living completely in its own world, and as a practice, people weren't willing to share business information.

But, even though it was way too early, I thought that using the information generated by the community to benefit the community, the companies, and the people who worked inside those companies was a good idea. We simply needed the technology and the willingness of people to share information to catch up.

WHY IS THIS POSSIBLE NOW?

Much has happened in the 20 years since I first had this idea. And those changes have made it possible to (finally) put the idea of Community Intelligence to work.

One of the biggest changes is the willingness of people like you and me to share information. We now live in a sharing economy. We do it personally—think of all the social media people use to share what is going on with them—and nearly everywhere in our lives. Uber and Lyft are examples of the sharing economy. So are places like WeWork, which provides shared workspaces; Airbnb; and services like Turo where you can rent your car from others.

Sharing is now commonplace. Just think of all the examples—both bad and good—of videos going viral. Someone catches someone doing something nice for someone, or someone in a position of power abuses someone, and the whole world knows almost immediately. Our society is more open than it ever was. That's one thing that has changed since I first began thinking about the idea.

And along with that sharing has come an increased willingness to connect and then to collaborate. We have talked a bit about that in the sense that all of us are smarter than any one of us, and also about the willingness of companies that compete head-to-head in one place to collaborate in other areas and then to end those relationships when there is no longer value to continuing them.

Given that the world is smaller, more transparent, and moving faster, you don't have a choice except to collaborate, often in real time. Few organizations have the resources to go it alone. And collaboration today no longer requires you to know who you are collaborating with. For example, in the collaboration I am talking about—Community Intelligence, where organizations share information—you don't even necessarily need to know another person or company. You are going to get insights simply because you are a member of the community. You can sightlessly collaborate just as you do when you have Waze open when you are driving your car.

This is not about relying on the wisdom of crowds

Let me answer two questions that I sometimes get when I begin talking about how the power of the community can help the community, your company, and you.

The first is "How is this different from crowdsourcing?"

Substantially.

And the second is "How is this related to drawing on the wisdom of crowds?"

Vaguely.

Let's deal with crowdsourcing first. Crowdsourcing is the practice of engaging a bunch of people (i.e., a crowd) toward a common goal of funding or creating something. So, in that sense, you could say it is, at best, slightly similar to Community Intelligence in that we are trying to create something too—organizations that perform better.

But crowdsourcing requires a member of the crowd to do something. With Community Intelligence, information flows automatically like it does with Waze. It doesn't require any action on behalf of the crowd, other than the willingness to have some third party monitor what the crowd is doing.

The second major difference: Crowdsourcing is not capturing the information of the entire crowd, only the members who are actively contributing. So, in that sense, it is like a Yelp review, where you only know the comments of people who contributed, but not of everyone who went to the restaurant. You are getting some data points, but not all.

"The wisdom of the crowd" idea, which gets its title from James Surowiecki's book, comes closer to what we a`re talking about. Surowiecki's central argument: The opinions of many people are, in the aggregate, more accurate than the opinions of individuals or small groups.

continued

However, the key distinction with what we are discussing is opinions. If you ask three people what the capital of Oregon is, they might say they don't know. So their opinions don't help you much.

And if you ask 100 and 73 say "Portland," it doesn't mean the answer is correct just because that's what the majority of the people surveyed said. (Oregon's capital is Salem.)

With Community Intelligence you get facts. The people who are participating are showcasing exactly what they did ("We bought 10 desks from Supplier X for $762 a desk). They are not guessing about anything.

Another fact that has changed is the speed of data exchange that is now possible because of both computing power and the internet. The full exploitation of the internet has also made us more collaborative. You can see it through social networks, online bulletin boards, and even gaming. People play games online with people they have never met, people who can be halfway across the world.

So, the first factor that has changed is the people, us. The second is the computing power. The amount of data that we are able to collect nonintrusively is accelerating at a rapid pace, and the technology processing capabilities that are available to crunch that data, and then distill knowledge out of it, have gotten dramatically better as well.

The third concept that has changed is software. We've been able to create systems that are much more agile and flexible. Now, not only the computing power but the actual functionality and flexibility of the available software allow the collaboration to happen.

So, data, technology, and people are the three fundamental

components that are shifting to create the proverbial perfect storm that is leading to this community concept.

BUT SHOULD WE DO IT?

It is one thing to say we now have the ability to draw on the power of community. It is quite another to say we should. Why should we? Let me start in what some people will think is a surprising place.

At our core, we are social beings. Yes, we have all of this technology and data, but we are, in essence, collaborators, and we have been since we were cave people living in tribes. The word *community* comes from the word *commune*, which in its verb form means "to converse or talk together, usually with profound intensity, intimacy, and so on." And if we are talking about *community* as a noun, it is "any small group of people who have common interests or responsibilities."

So, either way you use the word, we are social beings who, in the context of this book, are operating within a capitalist structure. That means we partner with one another when it benefits both parties. We don't do it altruistically. Rather, self-driven interest drives the desire to collaborate.

When it comes to the power of community in general, and Community Intelligence in particular, collaboration is important, as is the fact that it can be done with a minimum of friction. If the collaboration is cumbersome, if it takes a lot of time, and if we have to do it face-to-face—working out all the logistics that that entails— the odds of any collaboration happening are reduced. Having to coordinate calendars and go to a central location is not an agile (read: friction-free) way to operate.

But think back to the Waze example where they are pinging your phone once a second and you don't have to do a thing, other than be using the Waze app. That is virtually frictionless collaboration. You are contributing without having to do (almost) anything.

When it comes to Community Intelligence, technology is what allows us to pick up information without friction.

COULD YOU GO IT ALONE?

Occasionally, when I talk about the potential power of community and Community Intelligence, some company leaders—even those of high-performing companies—dismiss the idea out of hand.

The first comment goes something like this: "Yes, I understand how drawing on what the community knows could help some companies. But we are doing just fine on our own, thank you."

I think that's inside-the-box thinking. You don't truly know what's possible unless you open up your worldview, which is what the power of community allows you to do.

> *Drawing on the power of community in general, and Community Intelligence in particular, will allow you to do what you do better.*

It gives you perspective on the entire world of possibilities for your business. It provides more options to pursue, such as new customers you might want to target and different ways to incentivize your employees.

The second bit of pushback I get? "Okay, I can understand how getting the data from the community could make me better. But I am going to have all of this information flooding in, and I am going to be overwhelmed by irrelevant stuff and forced to analyze all that data."

I would agree, if that is the way it worked. But you should not be doing the analysis. You should be getting distilled prescriptive insights. It should work like Waze. You don't have to analyze traffic patterns. Waze does it for you and then prescribes the best routes. All you have to do is say, "It's okay for you to track my driving through the app." Once you do that, Waze does all of the hard work.

The pressure should be on the technology, not you. You shouldn't feel any pressure. You should get only value. And to get it, all you should have to do is share what is going on with you, exactly as you do with Waze.

Now you can say to me, continuing our Waze analogy, "Well, I don't have to do this. I've been driving this same route for 15 years, and I drive great. I don't need any help getting from here to there."

I have no reason to doubt you. But wouldn't you want to know that it is actually 15 minutes faster on Thursdays if you go another way?

By saying you should consider the power of Community Intelligence, I am not denigrating your abilities in any way. I am willing to concede, to continue our analogy, that you are a wonderful driver, but there are many drivers out there who are using some of the latest technology to outhustle you, and you don't want to get left behind.

To retain your leadership as an amazing driver, you're going to want to get the latest technology to stay ahead. Perhaps you are reading this book because you want to stay out in front of the competition. Using the power of community is one way to do it. That's on the positive side.

And on the negative side, by using Community Intelligence, you can protect yourself from being blindsided. That is no small outcome. Given the pace of business today, where product life cycles are much shorter, and new (and unanticipated) competitors can enter your market seemingly overnight, you want as much warning as possible so you can prepare, counterattack, and thrive.

WHAT DO YOU DO ABOUT ALL OF THIS?

Given everything that we have just talked about, what is a leader or an employee to do?

The easiest option is to embrace technologies that can make your business more agile and then take advantage of those technologies and the improvement they bring to improve your company. Use the information I've presented to foster collaboration and learn from others around you. Take full advantage of the power of community.

The rest of the book will be devoted to showing you how.

Chapter 2

MAKING THE
BUSINESS CASE

If you came to this idea of Community Intelligence cold and someone said to you, "You can use the information generated by the community to benefit the community, your company, and you," you might react by saying, "That sounds kind of interesting."

But from there you might also say: "It seems sort of squishy." And then you would probably ask: "How exactly would you do that?"

This chapter is going to be devoted to making the business case for Community Intelligence.

Working together

It's hard to disagree with this starting point: There is value in working together. That's how tribes form—like-minded people come together. Communities coalesce around what they have in common.

continued

And once these groups form, they benefit in sharing information with each other. So this concept is not new. The key is to be able to share information in a way that is okay with you—you never give your proprietary data, and you make sure your information is anonymized. That's the heart of it.

As long as those conditions are met and you are getting back more in return than you contribute, I don't see why you would not want to participate.

I can't think of a more skeptical audience than senior business leaders, so here's what I would say to them directly over dinner to make the business case for using the power of community to help their companies:

It is clear that every company operating in a global business climate—and that is nearly every organization these days, since competition can come from anywhere—is battling against multiple companies, yet we are basing our decisions on our own data and whatever information we can get from third parties who might be able to provide us with some insights we can't get ourselves.

It seems silly that we're all working by ourselves in terms of how we find customers, recruit people, and search for the different suppliers we need to help build our businesses. Isn't it crazy that we're all doing it separately and that we don't have a mechanism to share valuable insights?

What if we had a way through technology to, with virtually no effort, contribute anonymous information to a pool so that we could learn information from one another such as—

- Which suppliers reliably offer the best services at the best prices
- Where the greatest pools of talent are for the skills we're seeking
- Which industries are more likely to be buying this coming quarter

It seems ridiculous that you and I, in choosing a restaurant, have a better idea of where to get quality food at a good price in an environment we'd like—thanks to community-pooled data sites like Yelp and Zagat—than we do about better ways to run our business based on industry data.

That's weird, isn't it?

For example, had we known there was a real-time surge in information technology spending in, say, the retail sector, we could have sent our sales teams to go after it. But we didn't have that kind of intelligence, which could have improved our businesses. Wouldn't we want to have real-time access to insights like that? If we had a large enough data pool, with enough information to be both valid and statistically significant, it would be much easier to operate our businesses more efficiently, wouldn't it?

Like Yelp, but better

I previously mentioned that elements of Community Intelligence can work like Yelp, in that you can get information on suppliers and potential suppliers just like you can get the ratings of a particular restaurant from all of the people who have gone there.

But the kind of future I am imagining can go beyond what Yelp

continued

does because Yelp, or whatever restaurant-rating service you use, doesn't include certain information. For example, some restaurants automatically add a service charge to your meal—18 percent is typical. Yelp doesn't tell you that, but it could be important to know for some people who want to control how much they tip (and who would get resentful if they had to tip 18 percent for what they considered bad service).

Yelp could find out about that mandatory tipping simply by working with the credit card companies. (After all, it is on the credit card receipt.) Users would never have to enter that information.

Similarly, Yelp could easily find out how long someone typically stays at a restaurant by comparing reservation times with when the bill was paid. That could be important to know for optimizing restaurant efficiencies.

The point? We have various models for what we are talking about when we discuss Community Intelligence, and we could make the models even more efficient and helpful to businesses—and the people who run them.

THIS IS NOW THE WAY OF THE WORLD

We are living in an open world where, in countless situations, as we discussed earlier, companies are competing against one another in one place and partnering in another. A great example is Microsoft offering its apps like Office and Outlook on Apple devices. Ford and Volkswagen—long-time competitors—announced in early 2019 a plan to develop commercial vans and pickup trucks together, and to "investigate" how they might work together to develop electric and self-driving cars. In enterprise software, the trend is to have everything be open so you can hook up the pieces—no matter who made them—like Lego blocks.

This greater willingness to collaborate is something that millennials, who are the next generation of leaders, have grown up with. Their mindset is that all they have to do is Google something and the information they want will come up. People now expect to be able to find facts about anything. You're walking down the street, you're curious about some historical fact, you look it up. The world of information is available at everyone's fingertips. Hoarding information is becoming progressively more difficult.

Now, I do understand the potential privacy concerns and have, in fact, devoted an entire chapter to it, Chapter 4. But as you will see when we get there, privacy is less of a problem than you may believe.

GETTING DOWN TO BUSINESS CASES

As part of the high-level discussion of how Community Intelligence can help your business compete, let's look briefly at some specific ways it can help you improve. (We will return to this subject again, from a different perspective, in Chapter 5.)

Specifically, let's look at four simple ways Community Intelligence can make your company operate more efficiently—benchmarking, best practices, improving IT, and controlling business spending—and then foreshadow our discussion in Chapter 6 by pointing out what's in it for leaders and employees.

BENCHMARKING

You always need to know how well you are doing. When I was running cross-country in high school, the average time for a male my age to run five kilometers was 25 minutes. If I ran it in 22 minutes, I was in the top 10 percent. If I was under 20 minutes, I was in the top 5 percent. Armed with those benchmarks, I knew where I stood at all times.

> *We live in a relative world. You need to know where you fit in. And to do that, you need to have a wider data set to compare yourself to.*

But you can't objectively evaluate how well you are doing on your own. Community Intelligence provides the comparative information you need in real time across a whole host of different applications. For example: How fast is my company at approving contracts? How good are the deals we are getting? How quick are we at selling (i.e., how many people do we have to touch, and how long does it take to close a sale)? Are we paying our employees the right amount for their given jobs? You get the idea.

You need to know these details in real time or as close to real time as is humanly possible. That is, of course, not what is happening for most of us today. We are getting this information—if we are getting it at all—usually from third parties who may not be surveying the entire universe. That's a problem. And so is the fact that the information they're providing us is invariably outdated. It's rare that the data allows leaders to, in real time, make adjustments to their business to help them compete. That's no way to be doing benchmarking.

But if business leaders had the information in real time, and if that information was based on a wide swath of relevant data, then they would be able to course-correct more quickly. They might get into new product lines faster. They might spend less time on certain internal processes. They might hire from different talent pools. They might incentivize their teams differently. They might get better deals on the goods and services that they buy, or they might avoid risks in their supply chain. So, all of these components would get better.

Benchmarking drives prescriptions: Coupa case study

Having industry data allows the aggregator to not only share what they have found with all the members of the community who have shared their data but also prepare prescriptions based on that data.

When I think of the word *prescription*, I find it helpful to think of an actual prescription written by a doctor.

Let's say you go to a physician when you have the flu. Knowing exactly what to prescribe for you is based on a special combination of what is in the mind of that particular doctor—her education and experience, her knowledge of the flu and various bugs in general,

continued

and her real-time awareness of what is happening in the community. ("Hmmm. There seems to be a lot of this going around.")

There was no question in my mind that, at Coupa, we would apply the power of Community Intelligence to advance our mission to help companies use information technology to spend smarter. In July 2009, we began setting the foundation for this future by, in essence, writing our first prescription.

Looking across the entire Coupa community, which at that point comprised a few thousand users, we calculated the average time it took to approve a purchase request. We communicated this information to our customers through our platform, put it in the context of their company, and then added this: "The average time to approve a purchase request across all Coupa customers is 72 hours. In your company, it's 15 days. Consider removing some potentially unnecessary authorizers from your approval workflows to speed things up and decrease processing costs."

All that was missing was the "Rx."

Today, with trillions of dollars of spend data analyzed and millions of suppliers in our community, we can create much more detailed prescriptions. We can see which suppliers are doing the best job, which ones are not, and who the alternative suppliers are in each category. We also know what buyers want in terms of quality, price, volume, and a host of other factors based on their industry, company size, and purchasing history. We can bring the power of Community Intelligence to bear so that we can make individualized recommendations for our customers to consider.

For example, we can tell customers: "We suggest you reconsider working with supplier ABC Corp., because they have overinvoiced a large portion of the customer community during the last year, shipped X percentage of broken goods that had to be returned, and had Y number of disputes with different buyers. That's nearly 150 percent greater than the industry average."

Or we might make this prescription for a company: "Based on what you are spending on office supplies, you may want to consider consolidating to gain discounts. We recommend that you use one of the following highly rated (by the community) suppliers." We might tell another company that is getting virtually all of its supplies from a single vendor who is not giving them the best deals to consider spreading out their purchases among multiple suppliers to spur competition.

Of course, people don't have to follow our prescriptions. They can simply consider them as part of a broader set of variables they are tracking. But in any case, we are helping companies get smarter, based on the power of the Coupa customer community.

At the same time, we are working on creating visibility for suppliers so they understand how the community views them. Armed with that information, they can get better and begin to understand what it takes to be the leader in their market.

If everyone shared information in this way, it could contribute to an unprecedented level of openness across all industries, on a global scale, and we all could benefit—something I will talk more about in Chapter 7.

Prescriptions can be extremely powerful.

BEST PRACTICES

You always want to know how the best do it. Let's go back to my cross-country example. How did those guys who were running five kilometers—a little over three miles—in under 20 minutes do it? Did they do a slow jog of the course first to get the lay of the land?

Did they eat a certain kind of food two hours before the race—carbohydrates or whatever? Did they drink this amount of water but not that amount?

A whole host of patterns are related to what drives great performances. Best practices can be leveraged by anyone when you find those patterns. But first, you have to have the information to be able to drill down and find them.

Let me give you two quick examples. In human resources, you'd want to know your rate of attrition among the people you would like to keep. That should not exceed a certain number, depending on your industry. If your number is higher than the industry norm, it could indicate that you have a problem holding on to your best people.

In marketing there is a certain speed to the sales cycle. For example, you know it takes X number of days in your industry to close an offering that costs between $500,000 and $1 million. How long is it taking your company? The average discount is X percent. Are you giving more than that or less?

These are the details you want to know to find the relevant patterns and determine best practices.

IMPROVING IT

As I said, Community Intelligence is part of the third wave of business. Information technology is a key contributor to this wave. For example, IT vendors that embrace Community Intelligence should be able to understand which of their offering's features are being used most by customers and which are not. Clearly, if a feature is being used often, you can continue to fine-tune and develop it. If it is not, you can find out why so you can improve it to make it relevant—or you kill it. The key advantage of Community Intelligence here is seeing the utilization of a given feature across the IT vendor's entire customer base, not one customer at a time.

From the perspective of an IT user, the community data could help you identify places where you need to beef things up—you discover it is taking longer than the industry average to process nearly every kind of transaction, for example—and you will be able to see where, and how, your peers are using IT as an analytics tool, which will help you gain intelligence and insight.

HOW TO SPEND SMARTER

Having Community Intelligence will help you spend smarter. For example, you will know you are getting the best prices from the best suppliers who deliver what they promise on time. That means your costs should go down, as well as your risks of receiving late deliveries or less than acceptable merchandise.

Accepting that every company is different, by having community data, you'll be able to use various filters to figure out what's best for your company. While for you that may mean finding the absolute best price on everything your company buys, for another company, it might be the greatest reliability of service or delivery times—they run their plants 24 hours a day so they need someone who can deliver on a Sunday at 3 a.m. For yet another company, it may mean a supplier that adheres to sustainability practices or one who serves the community well in terms of local sourcing and hiring. Others might say working with suppliers who are willing to co-innovate, or those who are at the least risk of going under, is most important.

Additionally, maybe you decide to join forces with others in your industry so you can get the best deals through group purchasing. You have more leverage when you're buying on behalf of multiple companies, which is a community-based approach.

Benchmarking, best practices, improving IT, and controlling business spending are just four examples of Community Intelligence dynamics, and each has a compelling business case associated with it.

Now let's move on to a discussion of the potential impact on both leaders and employees and build out more elements of our business case.

FOR LEADERS

The use of Community Intelligence is an example of the carrot and stick when it comes to those in charge. The carrot is the opportunity to improve and dominate your market, which will lead to getting paid more and increased job security.

The stick is the ability to avoid blind spots. You may be thinking everything is going great, but perhaps you aren't comparing your company, your business operations, and your performance against anything. If you had real-time cross-company data, you would know for sure how well you are doing.

Let's look at a classic example: Blockbuster versus Netflix. In its heyday, Blockbuster was doing its thing renting videos out of its freestanding stores. And it saw Netflix begin to grow, so it launched its own little video-on-demand service in response. Okay, that's fine. But what if Blockbuster had had data much earlier around what percentage of people were switching to video by mail, and later to streaming? It could have adjusted its offering faster and managed the cannibalization process of its existing store locations with far greater control.

Without the data, you can rationalize any objection away. You can say things like, "How important is streaming going to be anyway? Everybody is always going to want to make it a Blockbuster night for years to come. Nothing urgent here!"

ATTRACTING BETTER EMPLOYEES

Why will Community Intelligence help you attract better employees? First, if your business is doing well, more—and more talented and skilled—people are going to want to work for you. You will be a company that is seen as being smarter and making better decisions, and that will attract a high caliber of employees because they will view you as being innovative and thoughtful about how you go to market.

> *Good people want to work for good companies.*

You also might be better equipped to pay the right salaries and have the right rewards and incentives because you have learned from the best practices of other companies.

For example, everyone loves receiving stock options, but in some industries what makes people really happy as well is flextime. At others, it is the size of their office, spot bonuses—a bonus you receive right then and there for coming up with a great idea or doing something that reinforces the company's culture—or free food.

You want to have as much data as you can in order to fine-tune your offerings to your employees.

FOR EMPLOYEES

You will be assured you're being treated fairly from a pay-for-performance perspective if you are employed by a company that is taking advantage of Community Intelligence. You will know where you stand in terms of your pay, because there will be compensation transparency in real time.

And you will also have data that will allow you to do your job better. For example, Community Intelligence might show you that a manager in your position is typically responsible for 12 people, but you only have 8 working for you. That could be a sign that you can take on more responsibility. Or the data reveals that it is taking you 14 days to turn around a request, where the industry average is 10. Clearly, that is an area where you might want to improve in order to do a better job.

Obviously, what "better" means will depend on your job. But by comparing yourself to peers in your industry, you will have improved intelligence to use as you try to become more effective and productive. You will see details like financial operating information (the budget for your department is $4 million; $5 million is typical, so it might be time to ask your boss for more resources). You will be able to see who the best suppliers are to use so you can save the company money and improve efficiency.

In sum, you will be able to benchmark your performance against your peers so you will know exactly how well you are doing when it comes to contributing to your organization's success.

There is one other potential benefit. Having this data could standardize the competencies or skills and knowledge required to do certain jobs.

BETTER STRATEGY, GREATER EXECUTION

Everything we just talked about—benchmarking, spending smarter (getting the best deal, not overspending), hiring better, and the like—will help your company move faster and execute better.

And Community Intelligence could also inform your company's strategy: which markets to enter, which ones to double down on and which ones to stay away from, and which core competencies to leverage for the future. It could point you not only to new products but to new places to compete. It could provide a better understanding on how and where you fit in the marketplace and how you can take advantage of what you do best, your company's core competencies.

A company focuses only on two goals—strategy and execution—and this is going to help you in both areas.

Let me give you three quick examples of the advantages that will come to strategy and execution.

STICKINESS

By providing your customers with access to Community Intelligence, you give them another reason to stick with you instead of going with somebody else.

You can fold that fact into your sales pitch. You can tell customers—and potential customers—that you will be offering them continued growth and value. "You're going to continue to get more value as you stay with us. The insights we will be providing will get better and better as the community grows and we gain even more information and processing power."

GREATER SPEED AND AGILITY

One of the upshots of everything we have just talked about is that you will be able to move more quickly. You'll have to do less research and rely less on outside research because you will have real-time information (from the community) at your fingertips. You'll be able to leverage everybody's collective insights rather than relying solely on your own and being forced to rely on outside data, which, as we have seen, is often dated and incomplete.

That means, among other things, that you can change course more quickly. You can move faster because you don't have to spend as much time researching. Not only can you move faster, but you can also be more agile. You won't miss opportunities, and that will allow you to better serve your customers.

Say you have a call center. If you know in real time, only days after you launch your latest phone, that 98 percent of customer service calls are dealing with the fact that when people hold the device in a certain way, they can't hear what a caller is saying, then you'll know almost immediately that you have a design flaw and will have to move the speaker location. There will be no need for a long or extensive review to determine what's wrong.

ABILITY TO FINE-TUNE YOUR OFFERING

This point builds off the last.

One important attribute of Community Intelligence is that it gives you objective data.

It is easy—and dangerous—to object to things based on a gut feeling. To use an extreme example to make the point, it was easy for the folks at the Yellow Pages to say in the 1990s as the internet was taking hold, "No one is ever going to look at online ads. They are annoying. People will always use our product to look up where they can find goods and services. That's what they have done in the past; that's what they will do in the future."

However, if they had had community data, they would have seen that an increasing number of people were researching—and ordering—online. It is more than possible, as we pointed out earlier, that the Yellow Pages could have become a force in online searches had they paid attention to the trend and reacted accordingly.

PROVING THE NUMBERS WILL BE BETTER

So far in this chapter, I have briefly touched on some of the gains that can come from drawing on Community Intelligence. But you have probably noticed that I didn't try to quantify the gains.

Let's do that here. Two of the most basic ways a company is measured are on revenue and profitability. Applying Community Intelligence can help in both areas.

The easiest way to show this is to use one of the simplest financial measures there is: return on investment. You know the formula for determining ROI. It may well be the oldest one in business.

$$\frac{\text{Earnings}}{\text{Investment}} = \text{ROI}$$

When we talk about increasing ROI, the focus is invariably on the denominator: How can we obtain our current level of earnings by making less of an investment? Asking the question that way makes perfect sense, of course, because it allows you to increase your profits substantially. It's a great way to make a lot of money.

Let's say your company receives $20 in earnings for every $18 in investment it makes. (Add a whole lot more zeroes to both the top and bottom lines if you think the example is too simplistic.)

$$\frac{\$20 \text{ in Earnings}}{\$18 \text{ Investment}} = 11.11\% \text{ ROI}$$

Your return on investment is 11 percent.

If you find a way to cut your investment by just one dollar—which should be more than possible as a result of the spending data you get from Community Intelligence, which will invariably identify places where you can buy the same goods more cheaply—and still get that same $20 in earnings, your ROI jumps to more than 17 percent.

$$\frac{\$20 \text{ in Earnings}}{\$17 \text{ Investment}} = 17.6\% \text{ ROI}$$

But remember, the denominator is only half of the ROI equation. Let's look at the numerator as well and ask how we can get a lot more earnings out of the current level of investment.

Well, again, Community Intelligence can prove invaluable in identifying both new markets and places you are already serving where you can get additional business. A quick look at our formula shows the payoff from those expansions can be dramatic.

If we keep current costs (investment) exactly where we started

($18) and manage to increase earnings by 10 percent (moving from $20 to $22), thanks to the new and profitable areas that Community Intelligence identifies, ROI doesn't climb 10 percent. It **doubles**.

So, drawing on what the community knows leads to both greater sales and earnings, and lower costs. I think it is pretty easy to see how drawing on Community Intelligence can increase your ROI.

Before:

$$\frac{\$20 \text{ in Earnings}}{\$18 \text{ Investment}} = 11.11\% \text{ ROI}$$

After:

$$\frac{\textbf{\$22 in Earnings}}{\textbf{\$18 Investment}} = \textbf{22.22\% ROI}$$

You only want to use this power for good

This is an obvious point but one I want to stress.

While the sharing of community data can be a good thing in that it can help all of us run our businesses better, if taken too far, it becomes not only a bad thing but possibly an illegal one.

Let's take a couple of simplistic examples to make the point.

It is one thing to discover that it is possible to buy pencils cheaper than you currently are. (You have been buying them for ten cents apiece and you learn there is a supplier who offers them for eight cents.) It is quite another for all of the pencil suppliers to learn that

---

continued

someone is selling them for eight cents and for every pencil manufacturer to agree from this moment on that no one will sell below
nine cents. That's collusion.

Problems like this can get worse. There is the danger that you (on
your own) or with other companies can unethically leverage information to the detriment of customers and consumers. It is plausible
to imagine a situation where some companies could improperly use
cross-company information to create monopolistic control of certain
industries, or certain functions or products within certain industries.

The answer to potential problems like this is simple and twofold.

First, it will be important that government antitrust laws are
upheld so that we have fair competition that benefits consumers.

And second, it will be incumbent on all of us, as well as the government, to remove bad actors.

Stan Lee got it right: With great power comes great responsibility.

ON A RELATED NOTE

A certain aspect of Community Intelligence has been implicit in
everything we have talked about up until now, but I want to bring it
to the forefront. If you draw on the data of the community, in addition to what is happening inside the walls of your own company,
you will be at an advantage over those firms that choose to use only
their own information.

What follows from that is there is an advantage to drawing on
the community data sooner rather than later. Once everyone has the
data, you can't, by definition, gain an advantage from the data alone.

And clearly, if you wait, you will be operating at a disadvantage against everyone else who has the information, which brings me to my next point.

IF YOU DON'T DO THIS

What happens if you don't opt in and start participating—and using—Community Intelligence?

The downside obviously is not short term. The risk is not this quarter. It's medium to longer term, and it boils down to this: getting massively blindsided. You run the real risk of missing fundamental, changing dynamics in your industry and as a result being outmaneuvered by those that are taking advantage of Community Intelligence to make their decisions. By the time you realize that you have a problem, it could be too late to catch up or change course. Think back to Blockbuster being blindsided by the new way people chose to access movies. Or the baseball clubs who were late to use analytics and fell behind their competitors that did.

To keep this from happening is one of the reasons I can see more and more industries sharing data in the coming years. I also can see more and more companies becoming aggregators of some sort.

Here's why I say that. Every business is becoming a software business to some degree. We are all becoming increasingly data dependent. So, to the extent that you're working with information technology as it's broadly defined, I think you should be in the business of providing information to your community. If you're serving two or more customers, then there has to be some information from the group that would be beneficial to the group. (And that will become even truer as you get more and more data to validate your findings.)

With information becoming increasingly transparent, it's only a matter of time until someone working with information technology will find a way to start sharing information among the community for the benefit of the community.

You might as well take the lead. You can do it because the business case is sound today. But you can also do it because it sets you up well for tomorrow.

Chapter 3

THE THREE KEY COMPONENTS OF COMMUNITY POWER

Given everything we have talked about, it is easy to see that, going forward, an absolute vital requirement for success will be having access to the collective intelligence of the community.

Why?

Because the old saying is indeed true. All of us are smarter than any one of us.

Let's now dig deeper into the concept of Community Intelligence and explore the three big pieces that compose it and the ideas we can draw from them to benefit the community, our companies, and ourselves.

Let's begin with the three component parts:

1. Data and intelligence

2. Information sharing

3. Collaboration and pooling of power

Let's talk about this at a high level first, and then we will drill down a bit.

It all starts with data and intelligence. Data is everywhere, but getting access to it if it is not inside your organization can be difficult, and you want data from outside your own four walls because the more information you have, the better the decisions you can make. Once you get access to data, you can properly categorize it and make sense of it.

It's one thing, however, to have access to a bunch of information and quite another to be willing to collaborate, to help generate—and share—insights from that information by exchanging it with others (getting what others know back in return). That's the second point. Are we willing to share? Or are we going to stay isolated and try to gain the insights we need on our own—conceding that those who share will have access to a lot more intelligence than we do (and as a result, have greater chances of success)?

And the third part of Community Intelligence? Asking if we can pool our collective power and perhaps gain significant savings, operate more efficiently, or perhaps even transform our entire industry.

Here's another (and more general) way of thinking about what composes community power: It's the people of the community (us), what we (and our companies) know, and leveraging that knowledge to drive results.

Politics is a great way to illustrate how the component parts of Community Intelligence work, although you will see that it is actually broader than that. But let's start by comparing Community Intelligence to what happens in politics. (And if you raised an eyebrow when I mentioned politics, see the sidebar, "But doesn't all the political infighting show we don't want this?")

In our political comparison, the data and intelligence part would be understanding the polling data. What issues you care about—it might be taxes and the environment—and what issues I care about, which might be universal health care and trade. We want to have a complete, unbiased view into the data (i.e., what everyone believes to be important).

Looking into the data, it would be easy to see patterns that cause people (us) to group together, share, and collaborate. Some of us might do this because we believe in gun rights, and we become part of the National Rifle Association (NRA). We might collaborate because we want green energy or a better environment (cleaner air and water and fewer pesticides in our fruits and vegetables). We might want to make sure we defend and preserve our individual rights guaranteed by the Constitution, so we join the American Civil Liberties Union (ACLU).

The Democratic and Republican parties are über examples of collaboration of some of the smaller, more focused collaborations like the NRA and ACLU.

And the pooling of power would be to ask what is in the best interests of the entire community spanning across different geographies. In other words, what is best for America as a whole? How do we deal with trade and with defending our country?

A large part of the federal budget goes to the military. We make that financial commitment because we want to protect ourselves. That spending is an example of the pooling of our individual power, as citizens and taxpayers, to create something that is important and meaningful—security.

But doesn't all the political infighting show we don't want this?

When I use the political metaphor to explain the power of community, some people say, "Our politics in America are a mess. Democrats and Republicans are not working for the common good. Yelling at one another is common. So is gridlock in Congress and between Congress and the president. Politics is anything but a role model. You need to come up with three different factors and not use data and intelligence, information sharing, and collaboration and the pooling of power."

But I don't think that I have to. The problem is not with the factors. The problem is with how our political system is operating today.

Let's start with the first factor, data and information. There is a lack of transparency in our conversations around political events. The information is not as clear as it should be. We don't have the data, or when we do, people spin it however they want. Let me give you an example.

We mentioned military spending before. People who think it is too high will say it represents more than half the federal budget. And those who think it is too low, or just right, will say it is a fraction of that.

It turns out they are both correct.

The federal budget can be divided into two parts: spending that is either mandatory or discretionary. Mandatory spending is exactly what you think it would be, money that *must* by law be spent. This category includes Social Security, which alone accounts for more than one-third of all mandatory spending.

More than half of the federal budget is devoted to mandatory spending programs and paying down the national debt.

When you move to discretionary spending, the portion that Congress has control over, military spending does indeed make up more than half, but when you factor the amount into the *total* budget, it works out to be about 16 percent, according to the Center on Budget and Policy Priorities, a nonpartisan research and policy institute.

So, yes, it is more than half of the discretionary budget, but as we just saw, that figure can be misleading.

This kind of nuance on spending data is not always brought out in (partisan) discussions of our budget. Instead, whoever has the loudest voice gets to push their data and point of view, which are not necessarily right or completely accurate.

And clearly, there is a lessening of collaboration. You don't need to look further than congressional gridlock to see that.

Because of points one and two, you get pooling around the wrong things. For example, in an ever-more connected world, we are seeing the rise of antiglobalization, not only in America but also in Europe. You don't have to look much further than the Brexit vote in the United Kingdom and the ensuing chaos to see that.

So, does this mean that the three ideas—data/intelligence, information sharing, and collaboration and the pooling of power—are wrong?

No.

continued

It simply means that they are playing out in an immature way. They will get better as information becomes both accurate and transparent. Once people understand that you can't go it alone in today's world, things will change.

As we go about pooling Community Intelligence, we will want to start in the simplest places where everyone can agree. Let's go back to our politics example. You might think that we can continue using fossil fuels forever, and I may believe that we need to move to solar immediately, and it is unlikely that we are going to find common ground easily. However, we both agree that defending our country is important. So that is the place where we would start.

You begin with the relatively easy stuff and move on from there.

It is no different in business. Your pooling would begin in the simplest places: saving money by combining your purchasing power with others to receive bulk discounts, for example. Buying cooperatives (Ace and True Value), like those that your local independent hardware store uses, have been around forever. It should be relatively simple to get companies to combine forces to save money, particularly with the best information technology at their fingertips.

BUT WHY THESE THREE THINGS?

The argument for the importance of Community Intelligence makes sense at a high level. But why organize around these three things? Couldn't we have focused on other factors than data and intelligence, information sharing, and collaboration and pooling of power?

Sure. People can come up with whatever approach they want. But I found this simple framework to be an effective way of thinking about how business will work in the future. And one of the reasons I like it is because the framework builds on itself.

To see why that is the case, let's begin at the beginning and look first at data and intelligence.

DATA AND INTELLIGENCE

We now have access to data that we were not privy to in the past. More of it is publicly available, and the internet has made it easier to find. Plus we are getting visibility into all that data, thanks to the use of AI and technology.

That's good on one level. But on another it is not. Why? Because data is dumb. Individual facts, statistics, or bits of information are meaningless on their own. For example, here is a bit of data that is indeed a fact: Bolivia exports tin.

Okay, but what does that mean? Do they export a lot of tin (and what is a lot)? Are they the world's largest exporter? Its smallest? Somewhere in the middle when it comes to tin exporters? Is tin important to the Bolivian economy or a rounding error when it comes to exports, let alone its total budget? Is Bolivian tin of high quality? Easy to mine? Do Bolivian tin miners make up a significant percentage of the country's workforce? (And again, what is "significant"?)

> *Data is worthless without interpretation.*

What all these questions underscore is that data—such as the fact that Bolivia exports tin—by itself is dumb. It has no real value unless organized, structured, normalized, and put through a construct from which some sort of insight can be drawn. Data is worth nothing by itself.

Yes, raw data is important, but as we saw in Chapter 1, there is too much of it to be consumed in its raw form.

What we need from that data is twofold: First, it needs to be unbiased, and second, it needs to be turned into intelligence so that we can get something out of it that's meaningful. That is the second part of our data/intelligence starting point: Intelligence. Finding patterns in the data and understanding who cares about what, what's important, what's not.

And the more data we have, and the better structured that data is and the more thoughtful we are in drawing insights from that data, the more valuable it is. A simple example of that is human intelligence. The difference between Einstein and the common person wasn't that his brain was 50 times bigger. It was the last 10 percent of incremental intelligence he had, compared to you and me, that drove society forward.

Intelligence does something else as well. It allows you to see if our second point is possible, if there are opportunities for valuable sharing and collaboration.

Wouldn't giving people raw data be better?

Some people could argue that if we simply shared raw data with members of the community, versus intelligence in the form of prescriptions that we talked about in the last chapter, decisions could be made even better.

Their thinking goes like this: If someone is translating data into intelligence, they are making a decision about what is important within the data and what is not—and they could be wrong. If you had the raw data, you might make a different interpretation that might give you an edge.

So why not share the raw data?

The first issue is privacy. It is often fairly easy in exchanging raw data—even if it is done anonymously—to figure out the source.

But there is also a second issue. Even though you are getting intelligence, say in the form of a prescription ("We think you should avoid Supplier X, because we have doubts about his long-term viability"), the intelligence should provide enough information so you can see how that conclusion was reached. If you are told a supplier is risky, then you should be given data that backs up the case.

And obviously, if you have information/intelligence on your own, you may decide to ignore the conclusion or come up with one of your own.

For example, we tell you we think a supplier is risky because there are a number of news stories out there predicting they may go bankrupt. Now, you may know the CEO or have an in-depth knowledge of their operations and say there's no way they're going to go bankrupt. That's fine. Following prescriptions is not mandatory.

As we will talk more about in Chapter 6, you are the one who has to make the decision about what is best for your company. Nobody is arguing that you have to slavishly follow the recommendations that flow out of Community Intelligence.

SOURCING OF DATA AND INTELLIGENCE

Shouldn't we be asking the people who are supplying the data to be supplying the intelligence instead? After all, they are closest to the data and have had a chance to distill it. Well, on the surface that would seem to make sense, but when you dig a little deeper, you realize it does not.

First of all, the intelligence you are receiving, by contributing to the community, comes from a cross set of data that goes beyond data supplied by one individual. That's important. Think back to our politics example. Just because you care about a specific issue doesn't mean there are enough people who will want to do anything about it. Something you think is extremely important others may not.

Let me give you an example. I was in La Jolla, California—one of the most beautiful places on earth—when the Gulf War broke out. And in La Jolla, there is this attraction to the seals. The seals come close to shore, which is great for looking at them. The tourists and the natives love it, but it is not so great for the seals if some human decides to interfere with them.

While I was looking at the seals, a lady on the beach was trying to raise money to build a longer buffer between the seals and people so the seals would have a bit more protection.

I wanted to say, "Lady, I understand you think it is important. And at some level it is. But do you understand we've got our citizens going off to war? And this is where you're spending your time?"

My point is that, just because she thought it was intelligent for us to spend our mental energies on the seals, it doesn't mean it's where the nation should have been devoting its attention as a whole. One individual is not in a position to provide broad-based intelligence. Simply put, you need data from more than one individual. And, in fact, the more you can get, the better.

I think people would provide intelligence, and not just data, if you asked them to, but as in the case with the woman and the seals, their perspective could be limited and their conclusions less than helpful. When we are at war, do you want to spend your time thinking about seals as our highest priority?

Having cross-company perspective helps eliminate blind spots. You get more visibility into what people care about.

In addition, if everybody threw out their intelligence, you would have mass confusion. Let me stay on that point for a moment.

I am not going to advocate for either political party, but the kind of confusion I am talking about is what is happening now in our society. People are throwing out much misinformation about the issues of the day, and some of it sticks. We are struggling to get access to the truth because everyone's simply putting out their thoughts, and they all appear equal because they capture an equal moment of our time. But common sense tells you that all of these thoughts are not equal in value.

When you find yourself in a situation where thoughts are swirling all around you, people tend to select information that reinforces their views, which isn't helpful. You can be misled. You could be basing your assumptions on limited data.

INFORMATION SHARING

Let's start with a simple example. You care about working with low-risk suppliers, and so do I. We could share data about the people we are using, pointing out who is financially secure and delivers what they say they will consistently. And we could also share our experiences with people who are not as good and those who we think should be avoided at all costs. The same approach holds true if we both care about lowest prices or working with sustainable suppliers. We share the information we know so we both benefit.

COLLABORATION

Now, the collaboration we are talking about here is not collaboration in the traditional sense of being face-to-face. But technology today offers us the opportunity to collaborate in real time, which allows us to learn from one another, leverage best practices, find like-minded people with whom to compare notes, and allow us to do what needs to be done.

Here is what is now a commonplace example involving Hewlett-Packard (HP). When you bought one of their printers in decades past, it came with a 150-page manual that showed you how it worked, and it also had a section on troubleshooting.

One day, HP finally woke up and said, "Wait a minute. We're not going to be able to figure out every possible thing that consumers want to know about our printers, and we are certainly not going to be able to anticipate everything that could go wrong. Let's set up a website where the answers to printer questions can be crowdsourced. We'll curate it a bit so that it focuses on the vast majority of topics our users are interested in. Then we'll let consumers ask questions and have other consumers respond with answers." ("I tried this when I was having your problem, and it resolved the issue.")

HP created a community that pooled their knowledge about the printers, a community that not only showed you how to make the printers work well but also could provide ideas you may never have thought of. ("You mean I can print two-sided photos?")

This sort of online data pooling is now commonplace everywhere, and what's nice is the information can be provided in near real time and with less friction. You are not calling some toll-free number and waiting on hold forever.

Another benefit that comes from collaborating this way is innovation. Because you are interacting with more people and companies, you learn about opportunities that you didn't know were there for your business or yourself. All kinds of new ideas can be discovered this way. And that's what society is: social sharing. You don't need to look further than the fact that Pinterest, an online site where you can share recipes, home decorating ideas, fashion tips, wedding ideas, and the like, went public with a jaw-dropping valuation.

As *The New York Times* wrote, after the company's first day of trading as a public company in April 2019: "The company's fully diluted market capitalization totaled over $16 billion, making it more valuable than Macy's or Nordstrom, the retail chains."

Now, what we are talking about here is a different way of collaborating, and because it is, it can be of great value when a third party helps cultivate effective collaboration, as we saw in the HP example. If you think about it, this is what teachers do in the classroom or a facilitator does in any group meeting.

COLLABORATING MORE WIDELY

In the situations we have been talking about, we were collaborating among ourselves. Pooling of power is collaboration on a larger scale. We ask how we leverage our collaborative strength to accomplish something that we wouldn't otherwise be able to achieve, or to obtain something that would be impossible for us to gain on our own. We are able to get government protection—the police patrolling our town, the military defending our country, and the various public agencies maintaining our roads and bridges—because we're citizens and pay taxes. In business, this collaboration could play out with companies coming together and pooling their purchasing power so they can get a better deal on office furniture, computers, copiers, and the like. But more on this later.

UNFORTUNATELY, THIS IS NOT A PANACEA

So, are we saying that Community Intelligence is the answer to every business problem and needs to be followed to the letter?

Well, no.

To understand why I say that, let's go back to the discussion of a prescription offered by a physician. This prescription is a starting point. It may need to be fine-tuned with the dosage being increased or decreased, for example. The prescription is bringing intelligence to you—the doctor has taken the particular data points about your condition, analyzed them, and by doing so turned the data into intelligence—and then you can combine that with your own gut instinct and experience to decide on a course of action that you think is right for your health. Again, as we have said throughout, you are the person who is ultimately responsible.

The same thought process should happen when you get a prescription about your business, based on Community Intelligence. You need to consider the information in the context of understanding your company's culture, your company's priorities, and your own vision of your profession in general and your job in particular. All of these together create value.

Blindly following prescriptions is not the right course of action. If the prescriptions were perfect, then you would be able to automate your job. And that's not what we're suggesting in this book. (Again, we will talk more about this in Chapter 6.) But while prescriptions are not perfect, they potentially enable you to work more efficiently and effectively.

What kind of information should you be sharing?

We will talk about information sharing in depth in the next chapter, which is completely devoted to the issue of privacy, but let me foreshadow that conversation here with a look at what kind of information you should be sharing.

It is obviously an important issue, given the European Union's General Data Protection Regulation (GDPR)—which deals with data protection and privacy for all individuals—and because of all the privacy breaches we have seen in the United States involving companies such as Facebook.

As you will see in Chapter 4, my starting point is this: It is your data, and you don't have to share a darn thing if you don't want to.

But if you don't share, then no one is going to share their information with you. You have to give to get.

So if you want to get information, what kinds of things do you give? What kinds of data do you need to provide? Since this will be our focus in the next chapter, let me just underscore here the sorts of information that you *don't* want to give out.

Obviously, you don't want to share personal and private information that you wouldn't want floating about in the universe, things like your Social Security number or credit card numbers, or tax information about your company. And speaking of business, you don't want to share anything that is close to a trade secret.

Let me make one other point to foreshadow next chapter's

continued

discussion. You only want to provide your information to reputable companies who, when they share your data with the companies you have identified, do it in a sanitized way so that no one could ever get insight into who provided it.

THE POOLING OF POWER

The numbers vary, but everyone agrees that business-to-business (B2B) spending is far larger than business-to-consumer (B2C) spending. Let me cite one example to make the point. B2B sales are projected to be $1.1 trillion by the end of 2020, more than two times higher than global online retail sales, according to ResearchandMarkets.com. And that is just online sales.

B2B spend is the biggest spending there is, by far, by any measure. So with more information and data available, and with greater willingness to collaborate today, wouldn't it be in the best interest of these buyers with trillions of dollars in buying power to find opportunities to collaborate and pool that power to get the best deals?

Of course it would.

Here's an extremely simple example of how it could work. Let's say seven hospitals in a specific area decide to collaborate. They come together to see if they can save money on the nonmedical supplies that each of them buys—linens, mattresses, serving trays, and the like.

The hospitals ask the suppliers they use if they want to be part of this group-buying project, and let's say three suppliers decide to participate after learning how much the hospitals buy in aggregate. The hospitals then pool their information about what they know about these suppliers—the quality of the merchandise they provide, whether they deliver the right things on time consistently, if their billing is accurate, and the like—and decide to award all of their business to one supplier.

By consolidating their buying power and giving that one supplier a far larger order, the hospitals are able to get better prices. Each of the seven hospitals thought they were getting a good deal before, and they were, but the combined purchasing power got them an additional 5 percent discount on average, resulting in millions in cost savings.

Even better, once the collaboration was in place, they could reorder automatically electronically to continue getting the lower price. Electronically supported group buying is something that has never been done at scale and could be extremely powerful.

One of the great things about this approach is that it doesn't have to be limited geographically. Hospitals from all over the world could team up to do this, and they could draw on suppliers who could be anywhere as well. And obviously, what would work for hospitals would work for businesses of all kinds.

Buying cooperatives have existed for as long as there have been buyers, but this kind of collaboration takes it to a whole new level with a lot less friction. Up until now, it hasn't been on this large a scale, with this much data and intelligence, and with this level of potential collaboration.

It's the next logical step, and it shows just how powerful community power could be.

So, you can see where the power comes from in the phrase "pooling of power" that makes up the third point of Community Intelligence. We get insights from the data ("Hmm, all hospitals buy stands to hold IV fluids given to patients, and this particular supplier not only has the best terms but is the most consistently reliable"). Then we join together to share that information and to collaborate ("I bet if all our hospitals decided to get their stands from that reliable supplier, we'd get a better deal").

The power comes from having access to a massive amount of data and information that is then distilled into intelligence and insights.

Think about the example we just used. Thanks to the data, we know there are a lot of hospitals all over the world that are in the market for bed linens or IV stands. We know, based on Community Intelligence, that there is an opportunity to save a boatload of money on them, because we know what the hospitals are currently paying when they purchase the product on their own.

The power then comes from the hospitals coming together to leverage technology and use their data and insights to pool-buy across their community (the hospitals coming together) to get the best deal from a chosen supplier.

This is the power of community using Community Intelligence.

Chapter 4

PRIVACY: IT'S YOUR DATA

In order for the information generated by the community to benefit the community, your company, and you, you have to share your data.

The logical question is, why do you have to?

The short answer: You don't. It's your information and data. If you want to keep it to yourself and keep it within your organization, that's fine. It's your right.

But if you do that, no one is going to share their information with you. You have to give to get. That's the first thing to understand. There is value in giving.

Why?

Because when you give, you have the opportunity to get. That's how anything related to any kind of community works—there's some level of reciprocity. Everyone needs to contribute if a community is going to thrive. Sharing is central to any community you can think of, social or business.

Most people understand they need to give to get. But invariably someone will say, when we start talking about sharing data, "I'm not sure I am comfortable having my information out there. I'm nervous about sharing it."

Well, what are you truly nervous about? You and you alone decide what and how much you are going to share. And you don't have to share anything proprietary, nor should you. To take a ridiculous example to make the point, Coca-Cola would never even think about sharing the secret formula for its soft drinks, especially the one that built the company, what we now call Coca-Cola Classic.[1]

Few other formulas fall into that proprietary category, and if they do, then you probably don't need to be worried about sharing because obviously you'd choose to keep them private.

Let's talk about four other concerns people have about sharing their information.

1. **"You are going to sell my data."** This one is easy. Don't enter into any agreement with someone who has the right or intends to sell the information you provide them—without you benefiting.

2. **"People are going to figure out the data came from me."** Again, if you are concerned about that, simply make sure that the data will be anonymized before it is shared with the community. That way you remove the fear that the information is going to directly expose anything about you or what your organization has done.

3. **"People are going to figure out stuff about me anyway,**

---

1 The formula for the soft drink that made Coca-Cola a global brand is kept in a vault at the World of Coca-Cola museum, a short drive from the company's global headquarters in Atlanta. https://www.worldofcoca-cola.com/explore/explore-inside/explore-vault-secret-formula/.

anonymous or not." People hear the second point and sometimes respond: "But my competitors are smart. Even if you don't use my name, certain numbers I share will give me away, and all of a sudden, the people I am competing against can figure out what I am spending on SG&A (selling, general and administrative expenses) or whatever. I don't want data like my ratios out there." There are three answers to that. First, if we are dealing with lots and lots of data from scores, hundreds, or thousands of companies, specifically finding out facts about your organization based on the data you provide is going to be quite difficult once the community numbers are released. Second, even if someone guessed that the information came from you, is the fact that they know you spent 21 percent of revenues on SG&A really going to hurt you? And finally, there are other ways to get that kind of information anyway. For example, you might be sharing it with Wall Street on an aggregate level, or your trade group could have it. People are working to get as much data as they can. The numbers might get out anyway. Since they might, don't you want something in return?

4. **"Things are not as hush-hush as you may think."** Let's return to the Coca-Cola example. Yes, the formula for their signature soft drink is secret and should be protected. There is no reason the company should share it. That said, it is pretty easy for anyone to figure out that the Cokes we all drink contain carbonated water, sugar, and some kind of coloring. And even if you couldn't guess that—and of course you could—in the United States, the Food and Drug Administration mandates that the ingredients of food products be disclosed right on the packaging, the Coke can in this example.

Coca-Cola understands all of the above and tries to turn it to their advantage by stressing the benefits and attributes of its ingredients. Here's what they write on their website:[2]

Here's the list of ingredients in Coca-Cola:

- **Carbonated water.** Approximately 90% of Coca-Cola is water. The carbonated part is purified carbon dioxide, which gives the drink its "bubbles" or "fizz."

- **Sugar.** Coca-Cola Classic's sweet taste (and also some of its mouthfeel) comes from sugar. Coca-Cola Zero Sugar and Diet Coke are sugar-free.

- **Caramel color.** A very specific caramel is made especially for Coca-Cola to give the drink its characteristic color.

- **Phosphoric acid.** The tartness of Coca-Cola comes from the use of phosphoric acid.

- **Caffeine.** The slight bitterness in the taste of Coca-Cola comes from caffeine.

- **Natural flavors.** The essence of the secret formula of Coca-Cola is its blend of natural flavors. This is the most protected and secret part of the formula.

So even if we took one of the most closely guarded trade secrets of all time, the ingredients that make up the formula for Coke, the Coca-Cola Company probably could disclose what it spends on carbonated water, sugar, caramel coloring, phosphoric acid, and caffeine and still feel comfortable. They would not be sharing anything

---

2 https://www.coca-cola.co.uk/faq/what-are-the-ingredients-of-coca-cola-classic.

that is going to hurt them. And I am not sure why they wouldn't. Their list of ingredients is already out there. (All you have to do is look at the side of a Coke can.)

And this leads me to a slightly bigger point: Over time, you have to believe that all information will become more and more accessible—or less and less proprietary, if you prefer. That raises a question. Since an increasing number of facts are going to become known, are there ways you can get a competitive advantage as an individual or an organization that has information to share?

My answer is that you should look for ways to take advantage of your information for your own benefit and for your company's benefit.

Now is the time to start thinking about how to do that.

IT'S YOUR INFORMATION.
PERIOD. FULL STOP.

When we talk about privacy, we need to start with this question: Who owns your information?

And that's an easy one. You own it.

I want to be as emphatic about that as possible. It's your data. It's your data. It's your data.

People are starting to understand the importance of controlling their data and having the right to choose whether they want to disclose it. Everything we have said in this book in general—and in this chapter in particular—is totally consistent with that.

To benefit from the power of the community, by becoming part of the community, you need to opt in. You need to *choose* to do it. Nothing should be done without your consent because it is *your* information. That's absolutely the way it ought to work.

But since you have that right, why wouldn't you use your data for your benefit? That is what we are really talking about in this chapter.

If you are a consumer, for example, you can benefit from sharing information about yourself, because companies will pay you for it. Really.[3] They want to know more about you and will give you cash in return.

---

3   This article from *Ad Age* (George P. Slefo, "This App Lets Consumers Sell Their Data Directly to Brands," AdAge.com, August 9, 2018, https://adage.com/article/digital/brands-agencies/314555/):

Although it's early days, brands such as McDonald's, Staples and GM are paying cash and purchasing data direct from consumer, giving literal meaning toward the notion that "data is the new currency."

Between regulations such as GDPR [The General Data Protection Regulation is a ruling intended to protect the data of citizens within the European Union] and scandals like those plaguing Facebook, consumers are aware more than ever of the so-called value exchange when using online services. At the same time, they're also tuning in on how companies such as Cambridge Analytica [which obtained personal information from about 87 million Facebook users during the 2016 presidential campaign] are plundering their data without their consent.

To that end, Freckle IoT recently launched Killi, an app that makes explicit the value of data by actually paying consumers with cash for sharing their data, location, or providing insight about what ads they'd like to see. Even more money is on the table if users scan the back of their driver's license with their phones, for example.

Killi has so far lined up McDonald's, GM, Danone and Staples as participating brands, it says.

In the case of B2B or B2C, you can share information for the benefit of your company or to improve your personal performance at work, because the vendor who is aggregating the data is providing you with valuable insights in return.

But again, I want to be explicit in saying you own the data. You don't have to give it to anyone.

However, the converse of that is also true. Since it is your information, if you want to share it—to get insights in return that you would not otherwise have, such as how you stack up against others or who the best suppliers are and the like—then you have the right to do so, and that can be great because of the understanding, awareness, and information you will get in return.

This is especially true if the data you receive goes beyond simple industry information and actually contains prescriptions on how you might improve, as we have talked about before. Based on your spending patterns, you might hear "Try to consolidate your purchases with fewer suppliers—and we think X, Y, and Z companies are probably the best fit for you—so that you can receive volume discounts that average 4 percent savings for companies like yours."

If you have all of your own data and you don't do anything with it, how is it an asset?

Here's another way of looking at it. Since you have all of this data about your company—what you are buying and from whom, what you are spending in various areas such as people and technology, and how long it takes you to accomplish administrative tasks (information that is not always readily transparent at a company-wide level but can be found with a little bit of work)—the question is, can you get some additional benefit or value out of that information?

You own your data, and that's wonderful. The question is, can you get some value out of it?

THE TRUST FACTOR

Obviously, you need to trust the company to whom you are giving your information. You need to believe that they are going to do what they say they are going to do—anonymize the data so that people can't tell it is coming from you, and give you insights that you would not have otherwise based on the aggregated data from the community—and won't do what they promised not to do (sell or disclose your data, or reveal who you are).

Implicit in this discussion is that you shouldn't trust your data to just any company. You want to share it with a brand that is known for providing customers with value for sharing their data. You probably don't want to be a first mover in this area.

And then when you begin to share, you should start with sharing information that has extremely low risk, such as what you are spending on office supplies. (See "Hierarchy of sharing.")

Hierarchy of sharing

What exactly do you share? And in what order?

I get those questions a lot. I think you should follow a hierarchy. You start at the outer fringes of what is important to your business and work in toward the core. You then get as close as you can to the core of your business without disclosing anything proprietary in order to receive valuable information and insights in return.

Let's walk through the way this could work.

Say you are a manufacturing company. Since you are going to begin by offering the things furthest from your core competency, I think you could begin by sharing anonymized information about the indirect goods and services you buy.

Why begin there? The answer is twofold.

First, there is virtually no harm in disclosing the information. It has almost nothing to do with what you do best, and in return you are going to find out who has the best prices on what you are buying and who provides the best service—fastest delivery at the lowest cost with fewest errors. It could be an easy way to save some money and operate more efficiently with little risk.

From there, I would share certain employee-related data, such as who supplies your benefits like health insurance and handles the company's retirement accounts, how much you pay your employees, and what percentage of your revenues is spent on personnel, so you can fine-tune your recruiting practices with the information you get in return.

The next level up would be sharing a certain type of customer information—which industry set is buying from you. You want to do that because the information you get back will show what geographic areas to consider targeting. Now, if you believe that having a disproportionate amount of your sales coming from the Northeast, for example, gives you a proprietary edge, then you shouldn't share the customer information. Again, the rule is always this: If you truly believe a piece of information is central to your business, then you shouldn't share it.

Speaking of information you wouldn't want to share, you should not share the distinct manufacturing process of the products you make, whether it's rockets or raisin bran. If you have a financial

continued

services firm, you wouldn't share your trading platform, the software through which investors can handle their transactions. But I think you could probably share many elements around it: what you are paying your brokers or what you are spending on rent.

So to review: You begin sharing spend information, then expand to sharing data about your employees—if you are comfortable doing it—and then about customer trends, again only if you are comfortable. You always stop short of sharing details that are at the proprietary heart of what you do.

WHERE WE ARE

As you have seen, what we are talking about is trying to get your data to help you get better at what you do (while not being disclosed to your detriment).

Again, the benefit to sharing your data is you get access to a broader set of data to see how you stack up in your industry and where you can improve. And those benefits should far outweigh the perceived risks, because, as we discussed earlier, you have taken steps to mitigate them.

People need to feel they are getting back at least as much as they are giving in order to participate.

The idea of mitigation brings us to the question of legal agreements.

The act of sharing needs to be completely transparent. That means people need to opt in. And the way you get people to do that is to say, in writing, "If you want access to the community's data, you must provide access to yours."

There are two ways you can make this work.

One is to say you will never share the customer's information unless they agree. The other is to make the sharing of data the default position when you sign a contract with a customer (and making it extremely easy for a customer to opt out).[4]

(Most technology companies at the forefront of Community Intelligence have a clause in their contracts to the effect that the customer will share their data with the community unless they specifically tell the company that they don't want to.)

BUT WHERE IS THE EDGE?

Let's take a step back. It is clear that sharing your information could give you a potential edge. But does it really?

There are a couple of things you may be wondering about this.

First, if we are sharing our information with the group, and our competitor is too, aren't we helping them get a better understanding of the marketplace?

That gets us back to the discussion of the kind of information you want to disclose. Obviously, if it's the source of your competitive advantage, you shouldn't share it because that is what makes you unique. But you should be open to sharing any data other than

---

4   This happens all the time. For example, when you signed up for your company's 401(k) plan, there may have been language that said, "Because we believe everyone should save for their retirement, we are going to automatically take X percent [the number is usually 2 percent or 3 percent] from each paycheck and put it into the 401(k)." Telling your company that you don't want them to do that (i.e., that you want to opt out) is generally simple.

that—as long as the benefit you receive is greater than the cost of providing it. The additional information you will be getting in return for yours will make you more operationally efficient.

The second question pertains to the prescriptions we talked about earlier. For example, if you follow a prescription like this— "If you are spending 8 percent more than the industry average on personnel and your typical spans of control are two people fewer, consider streamlining your organizational structure"—and your competitor is being told the same thing, you may wonder if you really have an edge.

I would answer that question by flipping the scenario around. Not every competitor will be getting this information because they are not participating in sharing their own, so you will be ahead of those who are not.

Let me use my company by way of example. Coupa supplies spend management insights to 50 of the Fortune 500. That means those 50 companies clearly have an advantage over the other 450 that do not have access to the same data.

There are two other points to make about this.

The first is that your prescriptions are not your competitors' prescriptions. The prescriptions are tailored for each individual company—and are completely private. Your company's prescriptions may involve switching to companies A, B, and C, who are better suppliers—an area where your competitor traditionally had an advantage on you. You will end up with unique ways of improving, as will your competitor, who might be told of places where they could buy supplies more cheaply or that they need to speed up their internal processes, which lag industry norms.

That is the way prescriptions always work. If you have high blood pressure, your doctor is not going to prescribe the same drug that they would for your friend who has low blood sugar.

Do you want to be an aggregator?

Instead of simply sharing your data, you might want to be an aggregator as well. Your company could be a resource to others.

Why take that route? That's an easy question. You decide to do it because you believe—correctly—that if you provide the kinds of information and insights to your customers that we have been talking about, you will give them another reason for doing business with you. You will be offering them continued value and continued growth. As you collect more and more data, you will be able to provide greater and greater value. The insights will be bigger and better.

How might you go about offering this service?

There are a couple of approaches. You could start by providing a distinct initial set of data. In a tight labor market, for example, you might concentrate on employment data—what is the average salary for a chief financial officer in your field, how long does it take to fill an entry-level position in sales, and the like. You focus on something that is both specific and valuable to your industry.

Or you could target a specific industry segment, such as midmarket customers or firms that are growing at the same rate as yours, so they might be more willing to share their information compared to larger, more conservative customers.

Again, I like the medical prescription analogy for a number of reasons, and one of them is that while you may follow the prescription (recommendation) designed to help you improve, your competitors may not. That happens all the time in medicine. Surprisingly, nearly three out of four adults report that they don't always take their medicine as prescribed,[5] meaning they skip doses, take less than the recommended amount, or stop taking the medicine earlier than they are instructed to do so.

> *Community Intelligence will provide you with information that will allow you to act differently. How quickly you act on it—if you act on it at all—is up to you.*

So even if your competitors are getting recommendations—and again, they may not be because they have chosen not to share their information—they may not follow them. If you follow yours, you will have an edge.

BUT SUPPOSE YOU DON'T SCORE WELL?

What happens if the results of the shared Community Intelligence show your company is not doing well? For example, you are a supplier who is substantially underperforming your peers. If you thought that's where you were going to come out, your natural tendency might be to not share your data. Rather than look bad, you would want to keep your less-than-stellar results to yourself.

---

5   "Improving Prescription Medicine Adherence Is Key to Better Health Care," PhRMA.org, January 2011, http://phrma-docs.phrma.org/sites/default/files/pdf /PhRMA_Improving%20Medication%20Adherence_Issue%20Brief.pdf.

That is not the course of action I would recommend.

For one thing, you want to know exactly how your company is doing. The situation might not be as bad as you think—or it could be even worse. Hiding doesn't help you. It's only going to be a matter of time before people find out you are underperforming. You want to get ahead of that. Providing your data means you will be getting industry data back that will allow you to address your flaws before it becomes too late.

In addition, the prescriptions you receive could be extremely helpful in fine-tuning your strategy. Let's take an extreme example to make the point. You like to think your company is a high-end manufacturer, and you believe you are delivering high-quality products, but it becomes clear from the data that the market doesn't see you that way. They don't think of you as a luxury brand but instead as a low-cost provider. It might be a better strategy for your business to cut your prices and increase volume.

The reality is you want to share your information to get an understanding of how people are viewing your product in relation to the industry overall. These are things you want to know in real time.

IT'S A BALANCING ACT

Let me end this chapter where I began.

You own your data. You don't have to share it with anyone if you don't want to. But since there is probably less proprietary information inside your company than you might think, and more and more of that information is going to come out over time, then you stand to gain from sharing that data in order to get insights from the community about your company—and your industry.

The question boils down to this: Does the reward for disclosing anonymized information about your company outweigh the potential gains you will get in return?

Ultimately, of course, that is your call.

But I think in most cases it does—by a wide margin.

SECTION II

The Specifics

Chapter 5

WHAT'S IN IT FOR YOUR COMPANY?

We have talked throughout—indirectly—about how companies like yours can benefit from drawing on the knowledge of the community, in general, and Community Intelligence, in particular. In this chapter, we are going to deal with the benefits directly and specifically. To avoid repeating what we have already covered, the best way to do that is to divide the following discussion into two parts—*strategy* and *tactics*—and see how Community Intelligence can help with both.

Strategy first.

I think we can all agree that being able to predict the future with 100 percent accuracy is not plausible. We humans are simply not capable of doing that. Still, that shouldn't deter us from trying to get as close to 100 percent accuracy as we can. And to achieve our goal, we need to draw on everything we know and can possibly learn from any reputable source.

For example, if we drop our cup of coffee as we walk through the office, we know with extreme accuracy that it's probably going to fall to the ground. I suppose there is a chance that someone could dive out from underneath their cubicle to grab it first, but the odds of that happening are pretty small.

So, we can predict with incredible accuracy that if we drop something, it is going to hit the ground. Cause leads to effect, predictable effect in this case, thanks to gravity. (Yes, of course, the world could spin off its axis for a second, making everything weightless, which would allow the coffee cup to be suspended in the air, but like someone diving out from under their cubicle, I would not bet on that happening.)

The point about the coffee cup is this: If we're able, with enough data, to find patterns of cause at scale, we can probably obtain relatively accurate views on what is likely to happen in other places as well. Community Intelligence affords us that opportunity. We now have access to extreme amounts of data about the ways in which companies operate. In addition, we have the computing power to distill and normalize that data across the different variables that could present themselves, and as a result of those two things, we can start to make far more accurate predictions of what will happen.

The takeaway is clear: Any company that is trying to make decisions in a complex world where there are so many variables and information is growing at a rapid pace could benefit from having access to this wealth of data—from every industry—distilled into insights that could help them run their business.

Without it, companies would be at risk from all directions. With it, companies could be proactive instead of reactive. For example, if you knew the office floors were wet, you could have prevented that coffee spill. (You wouldn't walk there with the coffee in the first place.)

That's how Community Intelligence can help with risk—it allows you to minimize it. The community could communicate that the floor was slippery by posting signs warning of a wet floor. On the reward side, the company could take steps that would allow it to optimize its opportunities in a given marketplace.

As you can see, Community Intelligence allows you to be both reactive and proactive.

Let's look at another example, involving sales, to hammer home the point. If we knew that the manufacturing industry was slowing down across the board—sales were dropping and companies in the sector were cutting back on their spending—what could we do with that Community Intelligence?

Reactively, we would try to close any pending deals as quickly as possible, given the slowdown we are seeing. Even if we had to offer a greater discount than we anticipated, it would be worth it to take a bit less because we would be worried that otherwise the deal would not get done.

Proactively, we would start targeting other industries where the data showed firms were more willing to spend.

> *Having Community Intelligence is about as close as any of us will ever get to having a superpower. It allows us to see the future.*

Why haven't we been able to act on Community Intelligence before? Three reasons: a lack of access to all of the data, the fact that the data we did have might have been suspect, and (as touched on earlier in the book) a lack of power to crunch all the numbers.

Let's take those factors one at a time.

1. **We simply did not have centralized data collection**. It's not that the data didn't exist, but each company stored their own information, making it extremely difficult to get access to—and make sense of—a wide cross-company data set. You can't analyze what you don't have.

2. **Even if you could get the data, it was hard to get insights from it, because it might have been incomplete or organized in a way that didn't allow easy access.** Maybe the easiest analogy is Myspace and Facebook. Myspace allowed anyone to create their own site and have it look the way they wanted, and the site's overall structure was completely

customizable. Facebook, privacy challenges aside, structured the data on its site in such a way that you could understand information across an extremely wide set of users.

3. **The speed to collect and process massive amounts of data was not there.** Where we were 20 years ago is quite different than where we are today, technology-wise. Today, we can process terabytes of data quickly and easily.

Here's another way of thinking about this. "Today," according to Northeastern University, "the smartphone in your pocket has more computing power than all of NASA when it put the first men on the moon in 1969."[6]

WE WANT THE RIGHT DATA TO HELP PREDICT THE FUTURE

Remember that all data is not created equally. You want to use leading indicators—what people are going to do in the future—if you can, as opposed to trailing ones (i.e., what they have done in the past).

Why?

Because you want to use data that has the greatest likelihood of predicting what will happen. As they say all the time in investing, past performance is no guarantee of future results.

Having information about what is going to happen is so important because that is how companies—and employees—are evaluated. It is based on what you—and your company—will do going

---

6 "Is Your Cell Phone More Powerful Than NASA's Apollo Guidance Computer?" Science 2.0, July 5, 2019, https://www.science20.com/the_conversation/is_your_cell _phone_more_powerful_than_nasas_apollo_guidance_computer-239388.

forward. In a *Harvard Business Review* article, Gail McGovern, David Court, John A. Quelch, and Blair Crawford write: "The presumption of organic growth is baked into companies' stock value. If you decompose the stock prices of the leading consumer product companies [for example], you'll see that future growth accounts for as much as 54 percent of the stocks' total value."[7]

That concept shouldn't be surprising. After all, the current value of any company is 100 percent based on counting back all that is anticipated in the future into today's terms (i.e., the net present value).

So, you absolutely need to be living in the future and trying to improve your company's fortunes. That's why you want to rely on leading indicators, and not lagging ones, whenever possible. (We will return to the idea in detail in Chapter 7.)

FRAMING STRATEGY

One way you can use Community Intelligence to frame your strategy is by benchmarking yourself against others in your industry, others in your geographic region, and others in your market. That would include the incumbents as well as the new entrants to understand how you compare.

Benchmarking gives you an accurate picture of where you stand as an organization, which then allows you to make trade-off decisions around which core competencies you want to double down

---

7   Gail McGovern, David Court, John Quelch, Blair Crawford, "Bringing Customers into the Boardroom," *Harvard Business Review*, November 2004, https://hbr .org/2004/11/bringing-customers-into-the-boardroom.

on—which strengths you want to exploit to their fullest—and which weaknesses you might want to shore up.

Let's say when you benchmark your company against the competition, you discover that you are best at product innovation, specifically the speed at which you can go from idea to getting the product into the marketplace. That's important to know. As a result, you might partner with marketing firms to support that product once it's on the shelf, an area where you are not as strong.

> *Benchmarking will put your company in the position to better understand its core competencies.*

Conversely, if the benchmarking shows that you are great at marketing, you might want to outsource product development—research, beta testing, and the like.

On a related point, Community Intelligence can highlight areas you may have missed. Let's take a sales example. If the data is pointing to a tremendous revenue opportunity in a certain sector—say overseas—but your people have not thought about it or are not seeing it, then you may decide that it's an opportunity you want to pursue with much more rigor.

The net takeaway of this discussion: Community Intelligence will help you either concentrate on the core competencies you have or help you develop the competencies that you need going forward to compete effectively. Both of these concepts add up to what business is really all about. If you're an existing business, you need to be focused on what you do best—your core competencies.

DOUBLE-CHECK YOUR WORK

Even if you think you have everything under control and have a good handle on the future, it would be foolish not to at least double-check your own instincts, your own business plans, your own structure, your own board agenda, and so on against the available Community Intelligence, just to be absolutely sure.

How often should you be checking? I would say once a quarter at a minimum.

Now, the information we are talking about here can be used more granularly as well.

Let's start with hiring. Once you have a better understanding of, let's say, your core competencies—thanks to Community Intelligence—your hiring profiles might change. For example, you may find that you need more generalists and start hiring more liberal arts majors as opposed to people with more technical backgrounds.

But the data from the community might show the opposite. For example, if you see your industry is hiring an increased percentage of electrical engineers, it could clue you in that others are fine-tuning their value proposition. Think about the number of companies hiring folks out of computer engineering programs today. One of the reasons they are doing so is to figure out if blockchain is just noise or if there is something there. Right now, I would say no one really knows. But if you see others in your space are working hard to find out—thanks to the rich Community Intelligence you are receiving that shows companies in your field are starting to hire blockchain experts—then it raises the question of whether you might want to do that as well.

The parallel to blockchain would be what happened in the brokerage industry starting in the 1970s (and continues to this day). Nearly 50 years ago, Wall Street firms began hiring people with strong math and statistical research backgrounds—but no brokerage experience—to conduct extensive quantitative analysis, to supplement the research that was typically done to determine the value of a security.

As access to more and more data increased in the coming decades, these firms hired more of these people and expanded their roles to have them, among other things, create trading algorithms—when to buy or sell a stock—and even completely new products such as derivatives. If you saw that emerging trend back in the 1970s and '80s when you were conducting your brokerage business in the traditional way, you might have rethought your strategy.

But the change brought about by Community Intelligence need not be that severe. It could lead you, for example, to "just" change what you are offering in the way of compensation to your employees. If you're seeing that the industry is much more focused on fixed salaries for certain roles versus incentive compensation, that'll help you define your hiring strategy. If you're seeing the industry is more focused on perks and vacation time, you might want to consider beefing up those things as well.

So Community Intelligence can have a big influence on hiring.

And it can have a great impact on marketing as well. Let's take one quick example. Say the Community Intelligence gives you, among other things, the average amount spent on advertising in your industry. You see that your competitors are spending a lot on search engine optimization to ensure their name pops up when someone does a Google search for their product or service, so that gives you something to think about.

After you do, you might decide to double down on that area as well. Or you could say, "I'm going to try to do something different and creative and maybe do long-form TV ads, since no one else is anymore."

The takeaway is clear: How marketing money is spent by category in your industry should give you insights into how to think about your marketing spending.

What's intriguing here is that what we are doing by applying Community Intelligence to areas like hiring and marketing is what the world has always done when it comes to finance. The data there is already unlocked in financial statements, and the world has analysts and others who do all that data crunching. There's a massive industry trying to understand all those numbers.

True, it is a lagging indicator. We are only seeing those numbers after the fact, after the company has closed their books for the quarter—or the year, in the case of annual reports. But the idea is the same and has been around for a long time.

HOW MUCH WEIGHT DO YOU GIVE IT?

Let's move on to the tactical discussion and start at the highest level by asking: How much weight should you give to Community Intelligence?

The answer is that it is situation and context specific. The beauty of this discussion, as we will explore in detail in the next chapter, is that, even with Community Intelligence, humans—you and me—will continue to control the decision-making process. It's like the prescriptions that we discussed earlier. Just because your doctor gives you one doesn't mean you have to follow it.

Now, this raises another question: What happens when there is a conflict between what Community Intelligence reveals and what your internal intelligence is showing?

Well, you could dismiss the conflict out of hand, saying you know best, but that would just be silly. It would negate the reason that you have Community Intelligence data in the first place (to give you additional insights into what is going on in your industry). When there is a conflict, it behooves you as the professional to dig deeper and resolve it. After all, that is what you are being paid to do.

So when there is a conflict, you need to look at the data and draw on your own instincts and merge those two inputs to make a decision. The beauty of this is you will have more time to make this decision, because you will be freed from doing rote work—such as compiling numbers—because Community Intelligence will have done that for you, as we talked about earlier.

To see how a conflict might play out in practice, let's return to the conversation about core competencies.

Let's assume your company has always believed that controlling the end-to-end experience for a customer was your greatest source of competitive advantage. You are the Apple of your industry. From design to marketing to retail, you control every step in the process, and you are convinced that your customers value the fact that you own the brand experience every step of the way for their benefit.

But industry data is showing that other competitors are going in a different direction. If you are Apple, they are Microsoft, and they have determined they will focus on the one thing that they do really well—create a phenomenal operating system and then distribute the heck out of it. They are not worried about being a retailer or controlling the end-to-end experience. They are going to make the best technology possible. Period.

What do you do in a situation like that? Well, I'd start by collecting even more community data to see how your customers view you. And if the answer comes back as "Despite your controlling every part of the experience, we see you as a product company," I would immediately start experimenting to see if that is so by dropping some of the customer experience elements in a few markets and seeing how the customers react. If the results show that customers aren't valuing the end-to-end experience, then it would be clear that you're not spending your organizational energies—and resources—in the right way. You would then be forced to make a decision.

Steve Jobs did. He made the decision to manage the entire experience for the customer at a time when everything was highly fragmented in the personal computer industry—you would buy your computer from one retailer and your peripherals from another, for example. His was a bold, gut-driven decision, and that's why the business world considers him so special, because he made that call on gut instinct—and he was right.

But most of us are not Steve Jobs, and there are so many shades of gray when it comes to making decisions like this. Today, most people have no data—or only limited data—when it comes to making decisions involving trade-offs. Community Intelligence can give you the insights you might be seeking.

Again, it doesn't mean you have to follow the insights you receive. If everyone has decided to move away from controlling the end-to-end experience, for example, you might decide to continue doing it to differentiate yourself, after experimenting in a couple of markets to gain confirmation that it remains a viable strategy. But either way, Community Intelligence has given you more data to help you make that decision.

HIRING, MARKETING, AND IT

One often-overlooked area that can benefit from Community Intelligence is hiring. Let's deal with just one aspect of it: retention.

Let's say you discover through Community Intelligence that your industry is having pronounced success (new hires are doing great work) and strong retention with employees recruited out of liberal arts colleges, as opposed to people who went to schools that emphasized technology. That one piece of information could make you consider refocusing your entire hiring approach. That's about as tactical as you can get.

You could see the same trend happening in marketing.

> *Not using Community Intelligence*
> *can be extremely dangerous to your career.*

The automotive industry, for example, has always spent an exorbitant amount on "spray-and-pray" TV advertising. They spray their ads across countless channels and pray that all of that advertising leads to someone buying a car. No surprise that Community Intelligence confirms that this is not a great approach.

Now, you as the CEO of an automobile company probably have an instinct that the industry is shifting away from TV advertising, but you don't know how fast. If I can give you real-time data that shows that 20 percent more automobile advertising in the previous quarter shifted to online, bringing the industry average up to about 80 percent, you'd have a serious number to look at. And if your marketing team says, "Oh, we're in the process of doing it, and we're at 10 percent," then you may want to make a change to your marketing department.

A true story will make the same point about how Community Intelligence can give your company an edge when it comes to IT. I had a meeting with the new head of one of the world's largest brokerage companies. In anticipation of our meeting, he told me about an internal conversation he had recently had.

"You know, I just got here," he said to his chief information officer (CIO), "and I don't know whether to give you 50 percent more budget next year or cut your budget in half."

And to be honest, I don't blame that new CEO. He had a nest of old computer systems, and he didn't know what was valuable and what was not. If he had had access to essentially real-time data (as opposed to relying on analyst reports that relied on potentially outdated and incomplete data) that showed that the vast majority of the people in his industry were rapidly shifting to the cloud, then he would have had the basis to have a serious conversation around what his company should do going forward. He could have asked his CIO, "What percentage of our IT has shifted to the cloud?" And if the answer was zero, that could have forced the company to take action—quickly.

Today, great leaders are making these kinds of decisions based on instinct—but few of us have perfect instincts. For the rest of us, it is far better to make decisions based on Community Intelligence, which provides rich, aggregated data.

YOU MUST REMEMBER THIS

Your job as a leader in your company is to command the resources of your organization in the most opportune ways, to take advantage of market dynamics, and to allow your organization to competitively win and reap the rewards of those wins for your shareholders and your stakeholders.

Bringing the best Community Intelligence to bear in making these vital decisions significantly increases the likelihood of your ability to make the right choices and deliver for everyone—and anyone—who is a stakeholder in your business.

Being late to the party could cost your company—and you personally—dearly. But getting on board early could allow both you and your company to thrive.

WELCOME TO THE FUTURE: WHAT'S IN IT FOR YOUR COMPANY EDITION

ZERO FRICTION, MAXIMUM PROFITS

To bring everything we just talked about in this chapter to life, let's imagine how companies, thanks to Community Intelligence, will be operating in the near future. The easiest way to do that? Reading the **quarterly report**, dated five years from today, from the chairman and CEO of (the fictional) Dressing You, Inc. to his shareholders. You'll see he touches on the four critical components for every business: **Customers**, **Suppliers**, **Employees**, and **Finances**.

Dressing You, Inc. Quarterly Report

Customers

Before I tell you about the best three months in your company's history, let me share part of a letter I received from Susan V. Hunter, **a customer** who lives just outside Kansas City, MO.

"I just wanted you to know that I could not have been happier with my recent experience with your company. All I did was log in and enter 'dress for formal business dinner' on your website, and

---

continued

eight choices, all apparently based on my recent orders, profile, and people like me, popped up. They were all wonderful and were completely in keeping with the look I like, but one dress was ideal. Not only the style but the price, consistent with my previous purchases. It arrived perfectly pressed the day before I needed it. And I don't know how you did it, but not one other woman at our dinner wore anything similar.

"I anticipate being a [happy] customer for many years to come."

Susan is, of course, just one of our millions of customers, but she is absolutely right. We created a unique experience for her, and we will continue to leverage the best intelligence to make sure we can do that (taking into account her wishes, tastes, and preferred price points) for her and all our customers in the months and years ahead, ensuring both profits and sustainability for our company.

Suppliers

Now we couldn't have created that dress for Susan without drawing on our extensive **supplier** network. By understanding, thanks to Community Intelligence, which suppliers had the best quality, best reliability, most sustainable sourcing, and the best prices when it came to finding the dress Susan wanted, our fulfillment process was able to route the order to the perfect supplier to procure exactly what Susan wanted and to make sure it was delivered on time.

We do this on every order, switching from one supplier to another and back again, suppliers who can be anywhere in the world, based on quality, production times, shipping costs, and options. The order was handled computer to computer, and shipping and tracking were done this way as well. All this was handled with virtually no involvement of our staff here at headquarters.

Employees

Speaking of our talented **staff**, because they are freed from doing what used to be the mundane parts of their jobs, like order entry, tracking, and the like, they are now able to use their time, talents, and creativity for coming up with new products and styles. Our employees are able to track both what our customers want and what is happening in the fashion world in real time.

They are spending their time tracking and creating trends, always taking into account global collective customer sentiment, availability of supplies and suppliers, and global fashion trends. *FYI: It looks like purple will be the new black in the coming months.* No bottlenecks, bureaucracy, or rote work are getting in their way.

Finances

Of course, our ability to manage our **finances**, from compensating our suppliers and employees to paying down our (minimal) debt, continues to be fully optimized based on both our cash flow and availability of funds, at attractive rates, in the marketplace. And again, all of this is being handled automatically, freeing our financial people to look for opportunities and ways to make us even more efficient in delivering for our customers.

Let me give you a quick example. Since our financial books are closed automatically each quarter, we have been able to shift several dozen people in our finance department over to different jobs, such as searching for how we can get a higher return on our cash on hand and looking for ethical ways we can reduce our tax rate. After all, as US Court of Appeals Justice Learned Hand wrote: "Anyone may arrange his affairs so that his taxes shall be as low as possible; he is

continued

not bound to choose that pattern which best pays the treasury. There is not even a patriotic duty to increase one's taxes. Over and over again the courts have said that there is nothing sinister in so arranging affairs as to keep taxes as low as possible. Everyone does it, rich and poor alike. Nobody owes any public duty to pay more than the law demands."

That helped to contribute to the record quarter I am about to tell you about.

But before I do, I want to stress we continue to build a valuable business for the long haul.

Now, as for the numbers, we had record sales, earnings, and margins for the three months ending . . .

Chapter 6

WHAT'S IN IT FOR YOUR EMPLOYEES?

Here's the overarching question we are going to answer in this chapter: What's in it for your employees, or you as an employee, if your company puts the power of Community Intelligence to work?

That's an easy question to answer, and in doing so, I am going to make two assumptions and also speak directly to the employees themselves.

First, I will take as a given that the better you do your job, the more opportunity you will have for everything from promotions to additional compensation. In other words, I am assuming it's in your best interest to do a good job, because you will get rewarded if you do.

My second assumption is that you are interested in developing your skills and staying on top of the latest business and industry trends so that you're not only offering a lot of value to your own employer but also developing as a professional, which will make you more marketable.

I have to assume both these factors, because otherwise there is nothing in it for you as your company decides to apply the power of Community Intelligence. All of the benefits would accrue only to the organization. But if both of my assumptions are correct, you will want to have access to the best information to make decisions on behalf of your company so that you can do your job well.

So, your organization's decision to use Community Intelligence is not another edict from corporate that either doesn't make sense or is simply and exclusively designed to make the company and the shareholders more money. It is a well-thought-out idea that offers something substantial for you as well.

IT ALL STARTS HERE

Perhaps the biggest benefit for you is that by drawing on the power of Community Intelligence, you gain an opportunity to take your game up several levels. In addition to getting a load of valuable information, you should be able to outsource some of the less valuable work you are doing. For example, instead of performing rote tasks like tracking down numbers, you'll be able to do projects in a much more strategic fashion and become the interpreter of the information that the community provides your company.

So, instead of simply collecting data and reporting it to executives who make the decisions, you'll be in a position to go to executives with well-thought-through recommendations and ideas based on the community insights. You will evolve professionally to the point where you are not only gathering information but also distilling it into unique insights that business leaders can use. That's what business leaders value. People who can do that are the kinds of people they want on their teams and the ones they promote and compensate at higher levels.

WE WILL NOT TURN YOU INTO A ROBOT

Now, just because you are getting the intelligence from the community and recommendations/prescriptions to go with it does not mean you are outsourcing the decision-making portion of your job. Community Intelligence does not turn you into a robot. In fact, it does exactly the opposite by giving you more and better information that you can employ in making decisions.

Let's use the medical analogy again. You see a doctor to evaluate a health issue, and she probably gives you a prescription for what you should take and do to alleviate it, but in no way are you outsourcing the control of your health. You aren't doing that, and you shouldn't. Having said that, though, you're in a much better position to make choices about your health after getting the insights of the doctor or another expert who prescribes certain actions for you to take, such as quitting smoking or eating better, to pick a couple of obvious examples. You don't have to follow their recommendations—and you certainly don't have to follow them in a robotic fashion. But if you understand you're at greater risk of heart disease or diabetes if you don't, then you may decide it makes sense to act on what they are telling you.

It is easier to make better decisions if you are armed with more data and can calibrate that information to your specific situation. That's the key here. You are interpreting the insights that come from the community data and acting on them. The interpretation and action are still your job, and you will be in a better position to do it because you can remove much of the confusion that was getting in the way of your focus.

I will use the domain of business spend management in much of this chapter to illustrate these points and more. Specifically, we'll use a typical company's spending processes to illustrate employee value creation with Community Intelligence.

Let's start by looking at supplier risk. Today, you have to go out and evaluate dozens and dozens of suppliers in order to decide which ones you think you should work with. It is a laborious task. If the community can do that work for you, by giving you insights into how well the suppliers operate—whether they consistently deliver what they say they will on time, for example—and about their financial stability, then you can spend more time interpreting the information instead of putting in hours upon hours collecting it.

And as that data—and the number of companies providing the

Community Intelligence—continues to increase, you won't need to spend time updating your research to keep it constant. The community will be doing it for you. All you will have to do is interpret it.

This sort of change is similar to what happened with the internet. You used to have to go to a library and open up different books to get the information you needed, information that may have been dated (since those books had been printed a while ago and things could have changed in the interim). But with the internet, you have a global community that is collating the data for you and putting it in front of you in some prioritized way that allows you to conduct your research faster and with more information. The World Wide Web contains more information than any physical library can.

Sometimes when I talk about this data collection, people nod as if they understand, and then they say, "But this is my job you are talking about, and you are in essence outsourcing a lot of it, if not all of it."

To which I say, yes, I want to outsource the boring, least productive parts of your job because they are holding you back from achieving your greatest potential. You want to work efficiently, putting in the most effort in places where you can do the most good. If you are a writer who grew up using a typewriter, you could continue to use it, but a word-processing program allows you to do what you do faster and better. You can make corrections and move text around with a couple of clicks. You can accomplish more in less time.

Eliminating rote tasks and outsourcing work that can be more efficiently handled by others simply makes sense. The greatest value you can offer is your intellect. This is not a new idea. As a society, we have outsourced rudimentary math to calculators. It's not that we don't understand the underlying concepts of arithmetic. That's not why we did it. We did it because when the math is simple and repetitive, it's quicker to use calculators, and then we can spend our time concentrating on what the numbers mean.

This approach allows us to be much further along in our value creation, whether it is designing a building or determining what we should buy. You are getting paid to come up with the right answer; we don't need to see your work. We want to see the results, not the method of getting them.

NOT HARDER, BUT DIFFERENT

We've been discussing how using Community Intelligence can make your life easier, and it will, but it requires you to do your job differently, and some people have a problem with that. But the reality is you have no choice. The hard truth is that if you've been doing the exact same job repeatedly for some time, odds are the tasks you are doing will be disintermediated with technology anyway (think robots on the automobile assembly line replacing people who had the repetitive job of welding the front left car door as it came down the line). So, you have no choice but to step into higher-level work. The question is, do you want to step into that more challenging work with the right tools to help you do it, or do you want to step into it without those tools? Those really are your only choices.

In addition, I think the potential downside pales in comparison to what the power of Community Intelligence will allow you to do. To begin with, you will have insights and information generated by the community at your fingertips as you go about making decisions, allowing you to instantly apply your own judgment to the data. And that can help you in situations that are either simple or complex.

Let's explore a couple more business spend management scenarios. Let's take a simple one first. Thanks to Community Intelligence, it becomes much easier to find out which suppliers have the lowest prices and which are consistently late with their deliveries or are in danger of going bankrupt.

As for the complex, knowing that a wide range of companies in your sector are prioritizing certain areas of spending over others will give you greater insight into how they might be focusing their intentions going forward, which could give you a competitive edge. Let's use an example to see why that is the case. Say you're the CEO of a retail company and you have noticed that your competitors are focused on getting the lowest costs on products they sell. You may decide to differentiate yourself by concentrating on driving down shipping costs by improving the logistics through which you source goods. Or maybe you decide to cede the lower-cost battleground and instead choose to beef up your inventory. Your prices to consumers may be slightly higher, but shoppers will know that you will always have in stock what they want, which might allow you to gain market share, as well as increase your margins.

Another outcome that could happen is that you could be exposed to different forms of value creation that you never thought of, thanks to Community Intelligence. For example, your company, for whatever reason, has not been paying much attention to sustainability. But when you look through the data, you see many folks in your sector are concerned about that issue. You may conclude that your company should focus on sustainability as well, and you raise the issue internally to your management with a plan in place. (See "Working and playing well with others.") If your industry is starting to care about sustainability, perhaps that's because the buyers are starting to care about it, so you don't want your company to be left behind.

The same thing could be true when it comes to manufacturing.

You don't want to be working with suppliers who are using child labor, for example.

> *On your own, you probably could come up with good deals for your organization. With Community Intelligence, you will be able to identify great ones, since you will have a far greater pool of information to draw on.*

All of this is on top of knowing which supplier to use—and which not to use—and being able to buy more efficiently. For example, Community Intelligence can help you find other companies interested in procuring goods and services similar to the ones you are buying, and you can join with them in getting the best deals for your organization through volume discounts. You'll be able to tap into contracts that you otherwise wouldn't have access to without a community that works together.

That means you will be able to point to how much more money you saved your company, a factor that is always helpful when it is time for your annual review.

As we mentioned at the beginning of the chapter, if there is strong alignment between your company's goals and how you are incentivized, then they're one and the same. So, your ability to be a better professional, a higher-value-added employee, not only helps the company but also helps you and your career progression.

EFFICIENT AND EFFECTIVE

As you can see, having access to Community Intelligence will help you be both efficient and effective. You will be more efficient because you will have more prescriptive insights into how you should be spending your time. For one thing, much of the busywork will be done for you, and that will free up (perhaps a substantial amount of) your time. For another, you will have insights into what your competitors are doing, and you can either decide you want the same thing—"Hmmm, everyone seems to be cutting back and watching expenses; maybe we should be doing that as well"—or go in a different direction—"Everyone is cutting back. Great. Now is the time to expand aggressively."

And you will become effective because you can use Community Intelligence as a checklist of sorts, to make sure you don't miss anything. You'll be assured you're not spending your time in the wrong places and instead are concentrating your efforts where they will do the most good for your company.

You will also be able to leverage proven results for both you and your company. You'll have the power of benchmarking. For example, you'll be able to point to the fact that you configured your systems so that your company has the right level of control.

Here's a simple example of that. Pencils are selling at $8 a pack at retail, and you have negotiated a deal where your company gets to buy them for $4 a pack. That seems great. But you put in a workflow where 15 people have to approve that purchase. The fully loaded price of having 15 people touch that $4 order costs the company $150. You just screwed the company. While you are feeling good about saving $4, you have actually cost your company $146.

I wish I could tell you that that is a made-up example, but I have seen cases of this in real life.

Let me give you another example of people who are concentrating on the wrong idea. Your accounts payable professionals may be extremely proud of their ability to process invoices quickly; it takes only three days or whatever it is from the time the invoice comes in until the time it's paid. But some of those invoices might be duplicates or fraudulent, and they don't even know if the company ever received the goods that the invoices are for.

This is another example of where Community Intelligence can help. If your accounts payable personnel know—thanks to the community—that a supplier has a history of double billing, they can pay much closer attention to those invoices when they come in.

Working and playing well with others

As we have seen, using Community Intelligence will improve your personal reputation; you will be viewed as a more valuable employee.

But it will do something else as well. It will improve your ability to work more effectively with others within your company. You will be developing insights that will be helpful to other parts of your organization—sales, marketing, strategy, and the C-suite.

The reality today is that employees need to be agile. Not only do they need to be able to constantly switch from one task to another, but they need to be able to work with people across the organization as well. The organizational structure is becoming progressively flatter. Things move too quickly for employees to remain isolated in work silos.

Using the insights you have gained from Community Intelligence will help you work across your organization. That will give you an edge in advancing your career, because you will be making your company much more operationally efficient.

IF YOU DON'T USE THE DATA

There is no stick requiring you to use Community Intelligence—in other words, there is no overt punishment if you don't. It's your option to take advantage of it. And if you do, you can opt out at any time, but—

- Why wouldn't you take advantage of it? You have the ability to retain your decision-making authority while outsourcing many rudimentary tasks.

- If you don't, you run the real risk of underperforming your competition who do use Community Intelligence.

DOWNSIDES TO USING COMMUNITY INTELLIGENCE?

Are there any concerns that come from using Community Intelligence?

Here are a couple of potential concerns, but as you will see, they are not large.

- **Issue 1.** You could potentially become too dependent on the data, and that could make you risk averse. Why? You could decide to act only when the data tells you that you should, abdicating a huge part of your job.

- **Issue 2.** On a related point, there could be a problem if employees blindly accept—and implement—the prescriptions that come along with Community Intelligence without any thought to the implications, sort of like falling asleep in the process.

This second issue is troubling on two levels. First, if you were to blindly accept every prescription, you would be abrogating your responsibilities. Second, you would run the risk of being taken advantage of. Here's another business spend management example. It could be possible that the company that is aggregating the data and sending out the prescriptions has a special deal with a supplier and gets some kind of commission for every referral they make. They might be recommending the supplier—and promoting them heavily—even though it is not in your best interests.

This is another reason why you should only want to work with reputable companies. But regardless of who you work with, you should always be paying attention to the information from the community, and you should be the one who decides what information to use—and how. Even if the information is reputable, reliable, and accurate, you may decide not to use it because it simply isn't right for you.

The pushback to that is going to be "Wait, you are sending me all of this data, and obviously you are doing that because you want me to use it. And in fact, if I don't use it, my boss is going to penalize me. He is going to say that by ignoring the information, I am ignoring best practices."

And the answer to that is that despite all of the Community Intelligence you receive, you have to be in control. For example, you do purchasing for a hospital, and the Community Intelligence data shows that you are paying more for linens than most of your competitors do. But a deeper look at the data shows that many of the linens being purchased by competitors are being used in the operating room, where people are under anesthesia and so, by definition, don't care about the thread count or overall quality.

Or maybe the survey results are showing that the cheaper linens are causing rashes and people are giving the hospital poor ratings when they are surveyed about their hospital stay. If you are serving a high-end community where there are many elective surgeries, you may not want to go with cheaper linens.

So, the decision-making needs to be retained in your hands.

WELCOME TO THE FUTURE: WHAT'S IN IT FOR YOUR EMPLOYEES EDITION

MOVING FASTER WITH LESS FRICTION

To show how Community Intelligence will allow employees to accomplish more in less time because they will be freed from tasks that add little value, let's take a look at how Mila Agarwal, the lead designer at the fictional Dressing You, Inc. (the company we introduced at the end of the last chapter) spends a random Monday five years from now. You'll see how she interacts with the four critical components of every business: **Customers**, **Suppliers**, **Employees**, and **Finances**.

Monday, January 13, 2025 8:57 a.m. to 9:41 a.m.

What the *suppliers* can't keep in stock

With her coffee in one hand, and a brown bag containing a banana and a bagel in the other, Mila arrives at her desk. She takes out her laptop and turns it on, curious to know what the "prescriptive alert" was she received while driving to the office.

Tapping into the power of Community Intelligence, she had programmed both her smart phone and computer to let her know about

---

continued

unusual occurrences, not only in her field of fashion but in the ones that influence it: popular culture, celebrities, and even the economy. When something significant is happening, she receives prescriptive alerts like the one now on her screen.

Alert: Textile suppliers (whether they sell linen, cotton, wool, silk, or synthetics) are finding it almost impossible to keep up with demand for three colors: saffron (a deep yellow), flame scarlet (a dark red), and classic blue (reminiscent of the evening sky).

The alert is followed by a prescription that suggests: **"Create innovative designs using these three colors immediately to optimize time to market, since others in your industry are planning to feature these colors in their spring and summer lines."**

Mila does some quick online searches and finds that saffron-colored clothing was featured heavily in the surprise hit movie over the holidays, and clips from the various late-night talk shows reveal actresses showing up in the color as well, if they aren't wearing flame scarlet or classic blue. The prescriptive alert is correct. If Dressing You, Inc. isn't in the market with these colors soon, it could miss a massive trend.

Excited, Mila leaves her office to grab another cup of coffee and rushes down the hall to the conference room so she will be early to a meeting that is going to be critical to the company's immediate future.

Monday, January 13, 2025 9:48 a.m. to 10:41 a.m.

Getting the *employees* on board

By the time her design team has assembled for the weekly meeting, Mila has scribbled down a list of questions for them. But she begins by sharing her alert with the designers and procurement specialists present, and she receives confirmation that the insights are correct. Nearly everyone in the room remembers celebrities or movie stars wearing one or more of the colors over the past month.

"I know we are scheduled to go to noon, but I am ending this meeting early," Mila says shortly after 10:30 a.m. "Connor and Charlotte: Take the designs for our new line that have been approved and print them out, showing how they appear in saffron, flame scarlet, and classic blue, and get them to me no later than 11:45 a.m. Kaitlyn: Make sure we can get all the fabric we'll need in these colors. That 11:45 a.m. deadline applies to you and Billy. Billy: Talk to the factories we typically use and see if they will commit to producing complete lines that include these colors no later than February 28. Beyond that, we will miss the spring selling season.

"I need everything ASAP. I'm having lunch with a big buyer, and I want to pitch him what we have, including our new designs in the trending colors. Thanks, everyone."

Monday, January 13, 2025 11:59 a.m. to 1: 54 p.m.

The *customer* says yes

The New American Café, two blocks from Mila's office, can be described with two words, "understated elegance." The mauve and off-white décor shows off the tableware and crystal perfectly. The wait staff of both men and women wear blue button-down shirts and chinos and are knowledgeable and unobtrusive, as is the classical music in the background.

Mila is waiting at the table as the buyer approaches.

He is smiling, as well he should. For the last four years, nearly all of Mila's merchandise has sold out quickly. Markdowns on her inventory

continued

are virtually unheard of. While it is true that Dressing You, Inc. sells predominantly online, more than one third of sales are to brick-and-mortar stores, and this buyer represents about half of that.

As they catch up, the buyer insists on ordering two glasses of champagne "to celebrate our past successes, as well as the one you are about to promise me."

Mila takes that as her cue to bring out Charlotte and Connor's designs, which highlight the three colors discussed in the morning meeting.

"As you can see, we believe, *actually we know*, these are colors that women will want this coming season," Mila says, "and I think the designs speak for themselves."

Apparently they do.

The buyer points to a couple of the 12 sketches on the table.

"I am not crazy about those two. But if you get everything else to me by March 1, I am prepared to say yes to a $15 million order right now."

"You have got yourself a deal," Mila says as they click glasses again.

Monday, January 13, 2025 2:07 p.m. to 4:03 p.m.

The finance department is happy

Back from lunch, Mila heads over to see the CFO. Ecstatic about the potential $15 million sale, she knows the company needs to place the order for raw materials immediately, in order to meet the deadline.

Her pitch to the CFO couldn't be simpler: "Can you free up $5 million today, the cost of materials, according to procurement, in exchange for $15 million coming in by the end of the quarter?" She then explains the deal she made over lunch.

Like most CFOs, Dressing You's is not known for smiling, but this time he does.

"I think we can make that happen," he says. "And, Mila, congratulations."

Mila walks over to procurement and hovers over Billy's shoulder as he clicks his mouse a couple of times to come up with the best mix of suppliers with the lowest risk, best price points, and fastest delivery times needed to get the job done.

"This will work," he says, pointing to the final combination on his screen.

"Great, let's do it."

Billy places the order.

Monday, January 13, 2025 4:07 p.m.

A good day

Convinced, correctly, that everything is under control, Mila heads out the door to oversee the last-minute details of the industry charity dinner she is hosting that night.

Chapter 7

HOW THIS CAN MOVE AN INDUSTRY

As we have seen, there is no doubt that Community Intelligence benefits the community and its members. But not all of that knowledge needs to be kept purely within the community. It can improve the greater good of its members, of course, but it also has the ability to inform an entire industry (and the general public as well).

Think about a neighborhood watch program. If a local one has developed best practices around how to keep its community safe, why wouldn't it want to share what it has learned with the world so that others could do the same in their communities as well?

In this chapter, we will talk about taking that concept of sharing the best community watch ideas and applying it to business. Specifically, the question here is, can we take the expertise of individual companies and expand it so that an entire industry (and society) can benefit?

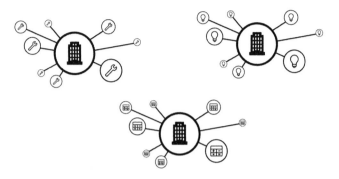

Getting information from the community will allow us to anticipate what is going to happen in the broader economy (see "Seeing around corners"), an idea we touched on earlier. Not surprisingly, when we shared this kind of information, there was a strong interest on behalf of the investment community to get access to this type of data because they believed, rightfully, it would be a leading indicator of economic sentiment. It is a wonderful resource to use when it comes to making investment decisions—which companies you should buy stock in, for example, or which companies you should target with your goods and services.

Seeing around corners

One of the biggest business challenges we all have is the ability to see around corners.

The best businesspeople seem to be able to identify emerging patterns ahead of others. That allows them to avoid or not get overwhelmed by catastrophes—such as when a new entrant with a radically new business model enters the industry and threatens their very existence (think about what Airbnb has done to the hotel industry).

You can see why this is so important:

- If you were making buggies at the beginning of the 20th century, you would have wanted to know your competitors were shifting more and more resources into the development of "horseless carriages" (automobiles).

- If you were working for the Yellow Pages in the 1990s, it would have been incredibly helpful, as we discussed earlier, to know other advertisers were experimenting with going online (and since they weren't planning to increase their advertising budgets, that meant that they would be spending less on Yellow Pages advertising going forward).

- And if you were in San Francisco pre-2009 and noticed that all of your friends were saying, "It seems like there are only four taxi cabs in the entire city" after they waited in vain for a half hour to flag one down, it would have been wonderful to picture a straightforward solution to the problem. ("Suppose we could summon a ride with a touch of a button on our smartphones from people who were looking to use their cars to generate income.")

None of us has a crystal ball. But what we do have now that can help us make better decisions is the power of community—and the technology to aggregate what we all observe and share it with one another.

As I have said throughout, there have always been communities going back to the days of cave people. What is new is the ability to collect the wisdom of the community automatically and distill

continued

insights in virtually real time, thanks to greater computing power and artificial intelligence.

By working together—by pooling our information as a community—we are in a better position to predict fundamental changes in a market before they happen. Instead of looking for insights solely within our organizations, we now have access to industry benchmarks and industry data in real time. That puts organizations in an amazing position to see around corners. That's what CEOs and boards dream of!

Let me give you a real example. Based on the aggregated and anonymized spend information within the Coupa community (comprising trillions of dollars of spending data at the time), we noticed in the first quarter of 2019 that there was an extreme acceleration in the time it took for companies in the retail industry to approve purchases on anything from office supplies and legal services to cash registers—things they needed for their stores and to run their businesses.

Seeing that the approval times were much faster clearly suggested that the retail leaders—retail CEOs, retail boards, and companies in the retail industry—were bullish about their prospects in the coming three to six months. They were gearing up to handle anticipated increased demand.

We could—and did—share that information/insight with the public, consisting of companies selling into the retail industry, economists trying to understand patterns in buying behavior, financial analysts who cover the industry, and the world in general.

This was an opportunity for the community—retailers—not only to serve itself but also to take its massive amounts of aggregated data and make it accessible for the greater good. ("If retailers think the coming three to six months are going to be good, then maybe it is time for us to increase our ad spending," leaders of other [non-retail] companies might conclude.)

And if you were running a retail company, and you had that information at your fingertips instead of having to wait to read about it after the fact from an analyst or government report months later, you would probably have responded in some way. For example, you might have sped up your expenditures as well, figuring your competitors had noticed something about a looming boom that you hadn't.

Or you might have decided to slow things down. The logic being that "if everyone else is being aggressive, they will invariably go too far and fight tooth and nail for market share, and by conserving cash we will be perfectly positioned to pick up the pieces when the battles are over. There are going to be all kinds of opportunities when the carnage ends."

Either way, that information about spending would have informed your strategy. You would have made a decision about the future based on the intelligence of the community. That's exactly what the power of community—specifically the sharing of industry data—can do.

It may be as close to a crystal ball as we can get.

The ability to see what's going to happen before it happens is a power that no mortal has, obviously. But we desire to increase the likelihood, as much as humanly possible, that whatever we believe will happen will actually happen. And to increase that likelihood, we need access to leading indicators of information and ongoing patterns so we can extrapolate how events may develop in the future.

Therefore, your strategy ought to be getting data from whatever, whomever, and wherever you can, be it the Institute for Supply

Management (ISM) reports—gross domestic product (GDP) and GDP trends, ADP payroll numbers, or Community Intelligence. And I would argue that of all the things I just listed, Community Intelligence is most important. Because nearly all of the data we have access to today is *backward*-looking. It is lagging in time. Even if it is good, it is telling you what happened weeks and, in many cases, months ago.

For example, with ISM, we get first-quarter information on what large companies spent on factories, equipment, and other capital goods around May 20 each year. And it might show, as it did in 2019, that capital spending was down 3 percent when compared to the same time the year before. But the information is reflecting things that happened months ago. There isn't much you can do with it in real time.

Community Intelligence tells you what is going to happen. No one can question that that is extremely powerful.

However, I sometimes get the question "Why isn't my own company's forecasting sufficient?"

Leaving aside the fact that the more information you can get, the better—having additional information is a really important asset—there are problems with the way that most companies' forecasting works. Think about sales forecasting, for example. The projections are based on what the salespeople say. If salespeople are forecasting fewer deals to close, then that would let us know that perhaps an economic recession, or some other downturn, is on its way. If they're forecasting bullishly, then that would, obviously, indicate that business is going well.

That sounds simple enough. But we all know that it is not. Think about how the data is collected. It can quickly become a game of telephone, as facts get distorted as information is passed down the line. The salesperson is interpreting what a client is telling him one way—he might be hearing "yes" when the customer is saying "maybe"—and he is passing that "information" (that yes) on to his boss, who will put his own interpretation on it. ("Well, if salespersons A and B are bullish, then odds are all the others will be as well, and I am going to up our forecast.")

Often, people put a too-optimistic spin on the projections to avoid getting fired or because they're simply wishing something will come along. Salespeople do that all the time. They sometimes put off reporting bad news for as long as possible, hoping, for example, that they can quickly replace a deal that fell apart. When you deliver news to your management, you want it to be definitive. Anything that is remotely gray tends to slow down your reporting, and many salespeople will see shades of gray in potential bad news long after they should.

But it is not always the salesperson's fault. The customer may not be telling the salesperson where they actually stand, because they're negotiating with numerous other companies and they don't want to show their cards until they've found what they believe to be the best deal. So they string the salesperson along, and that delays the reporting of what is going on.

On top of that, the data is not always recorded in a timely manner, and when it is eventually entered, it may not be complete, so you may not get all the details of the sale. (For example, it could be hard to figure out what kind of discount the salesperson provided, since the customer bought numerous things, all priced differently.) So you end up not getting a complete data set and make your projections based not only on incomplete data but also on other people's interpretation of that incomplete data.

Instead of all of these problems, you can work off of an accurate leading indicator in Community Intelligence. It can give you a good idea of what is going to happen in the future because it is both objective and *forward*-looking.

Let's take these points one at a time. Typically, it's much more powerful to use strong quantitative objective data to understand what is going on in any situation. For example, if a police car is on the side of the road and you fly by it, the officer is likely to pull you over and say, "Wow, you were going really fast."

And you say, "Well, I don't think I was going all that fast."

That's just two people's opinions on how fast you were going, and we don't have a clear picture of how quickly you were traveling. What does "really fast" or "not all that fast" mean?

But if the police officer has the tools (like a properly calibrated radar gun) to see that you were going 65 miles per hour in a 45-mile-per-hour zone, the data is irrefutable. He (and you, unfortunately) has the data that proves you were speeding.

So, if we can get access to that type of quantitative proof, it puts us in a completely different situation than having to rely on someone's opinion. For example, we can see that all members of the community, on average, are approving purchases 20 percent faster than they were a year ago. That's a fact. There is no interpreter bias such as "I think we are going to be able to close the deal." The bias has been removed.

Now, having said that, qualitative data may play a role, but that role is significantly minimized when you're looking at real data. The qualitative element (in part) is to help contextualize the quantitative information.

Let's go back to the speeding example. Let's say you know you were going 65 miles per hour in a 45-mile-per-hour zone. That is irrefutable. And the assumption of the officer could be that "65 is just crazy in our little town. No one should be driving that fast here." But you, the driver, may say, "Well, 65 didn't seem crazy to me, because I was trying to keep up with the traffic around me and they were all going faster." So that could start a dialogue.

It's similar to the salesperson saying, "I think we are going to lose the deal unless we do X." The comment provides context to the data.

But again, having objective data is the bigger point.

The other advantage of community data (in the context of business spend management) is that you don't have to wait until a sale is made and reported to understand what is going on. Virtually every company's purchasing processes involve a set of approvals, and you can track those instead. For example, if we saw that buyers were taking longer to approve a wide variety of potential purchases, not only would we be able to remove the potential data misinterpretation issue, but we'd have access to information far earlier in the buying process that would lead us (correctly) to believe that companies are less bullish about the future.

If we have a system where we can see what is happening with the approvals workflow, we can have access to much richer information regarding where companies are in their decision-making process. In essence, we'd have earlier and higher-quality leading indicators that would help us see around corners.

Would you rather look forward or backward?

Think of the way we usually try to figure out what is going to happen next in business. We look backward.

It sounds strange when I put it that way, but that is what happens. We look at how much the retail industry sold last quarter, for

continued

example, and then based on that trailing (after-the-fact) information, we try to project what it will do in the quarter ahead.

Community Intelligence is a leading indicator. It is based on what retailers (to continue our example) are planning to do. If you know in real time that purchasing approvals are occurring faster, you have a good indication the sector is bullish. That's important to know if you are a retailer—you know how your competitors feel.

So a key part of Community Intelligence is getting the information earlier.

Let's break down the purchasing use case even further.

Every company has a workflow they follow when it comes to expenditures. Let's say the IT department wants to upgrade a dozen servers. They could do it next quarter. They could do it in a year. They don't have to retire the old ones immediately, but they'd like to upgrade 12 servers, and the cost is going to be somewhere between $400,000 and $500,000. They've researched it. They've worked with the procurement team. They've got a great deal from a vendor, and so they enter the request into the system. And since it's a relatively large expenditure, it goes through a set workflow—the purchasing approval process.

It begins with entering the request, which in itself is a bullish indicator. The fact that someone senior in IT thinks that they're going to be able to get $400,000 or $500,000 approved in a given quarter suggests that they think the company is willing to spend the money, otherwise they wouldn't be putting in the request. They're not delusional, right? The only way they would enter the request is if their feeling about the company's willingness to spend is greater than 0 percent.

The request is submitted for approval, and in the world of Community Intelligence you can literally see the workflow, the stages that request goes through. It goes from the director of operations, who says yes, to the VP of operations. The VP of operations looks at the request and says, "Yeah, I think the outlook for the company going forward is pretty good. And we do need this upgrade. I think we are in good financial shape, so I am not going to sit on it. I am going to approve it immediately."

Then the request goes to the head of operations. Now, she has just come from a meeting with the CEO, who told her, "I'm a little nervous about the immediate future. I was just golfing with my CEO buddies, and they're all getting worried about the economy. Maybe we should be as well."

As a result, the head of operations says, "You know what? Maybe now's not the right time on these servers. Let's sit on this for another couple of weeks and see where things are then."

But then three weeks later, after reviewing all the data, the head of operations says, "Things are looking good—at least for us. I'm going to approve the purchase of the servers." And then it goes to the CEO, who is feeling better about what the review of the data showed, and the CEO approves it, and the order goes out.

If that process had happened over the course of a quarter when everything was bullish internally, the purchase would have gotten approved faster. And that would be a leading indicator of people feeling optimistic. But it took longer, so that meant there was some hesitation about what could happen in the future.

Today, we have the kind of data we saw in the server example in aggregate across every industry and every category in which you can spend money and across every type of company.

When you look at this type of data at an aggregate level, you can understand why speed of approval is a leading indicator. There is no potential for misinterpretation because you're looking at the facts. It's like our speeding example. It's mathematically correct.

INDUSTRY FORECASTING CASE STUDY: THE COUPA BUSINESS SPEND INDEX

At Coupa, we created a quarterly Business Spend Index to share with the world. There are three leading indicators or factors in this index pulled from the industry data.

The first is average spend per person. It is not what each employee spends; it is what the company spends on each employee, and the question is whether that number is going up or down. Are we getting people beautiful new Apple laptops, or are we buying them the least costly machines possible?

The second factor is the average rate of spend approval or rejection. This is quite powerful because we typically don't know what people intended to do and then decided not to. The only thing we see is what actually happened—after the fact. For example, we see—maybe three months after the fact—that a company bought 150 new laptops. That is good to know, but it is a lagging indicator that might lead you to believe that the company is bullish. But what we don't typically know, and we certainly don't know in real time, is that the request had been for 1,000 new laptops. That paints a totally different picture, and if the rejection rate is climbing, it is a confirmation that the company is increasingly pessimistic about the future; it's a leading indicator of less future spending.

The last factor is the one we talked about in the example with the servers: time to approve a request. Is that time decreasing, a bullish sign? Or is it taking more time to get things approved, which would be a sign of belt tightening?

> *You can make a good guess about what is going to happen in the future if you look at three factors: how much companies are spending on employees, what percentage of spending requests are approved, and how long it takes to approve (or reject) that request.*

Why these three factors? The short answer is they have proven to be the most reliable in predicting the future and allowing us to see around corners.

How the Coupa Business Spend Index works

The Coupa Business Spend Index (BSI), which we launched in 2019, is a leading indicator of economic growth based on the business spending decisions of hundreds of companies, across virtually every category of spending in virtually every industry.

It is completely behavior based and uses the three key spending factors that we talked about earlier in the chapter (average spend per person, average rate of spend approval/rejection, and average time to approve spend decisions). The analysis highlights confidence in the economy.

For example, in the inaugural report for the first quarter of 2019, the Coupa BSI revealed that despite uncertainty in the markets, there were sectors that were growing increasingly optimistic about the growth of the economy over the next three to six months.

Let me give you three real industry examples from that report.

continued

- **Business spend sentiment among retailers continued to be strong,** with the Coupa BSI for Retail increasing from the fourth quarter of 2018 to the first quarter of 2019, driven mainly by a nearly 44 percent increase in average spend per person. The Coupa BSI for Retail increased more significantly from the third quarter of 2018 (+18.4 percent), demonstrating that retailers were optimistic about the prospects in their industry over the next three to six months.

- **Financial services companies also showed more confidence about potential growth** in the next three-to-six-month period versus the prior quarter. This was mainly driven by a nearly 63 percent acceleration in time to approve spend decisions.

- **In the manufacturing industry, however, business spend sentiment continued to be significantly weaker** in the first quarter of 2019, as it had been in the second half of 2018. But, more importantly, the Coupa BSI for Manufacturing indicated that business spend sentiment may have bottomed out in the fourth quarter of 2018 with a slight improvement of 5.1 percent in the first quarter of 2019, showing that things were improving.

Twenty-four hours after the release of the Coupa BSI, the US GDP numbers were announced, and they topped expectations. The Coupa BSI proved to be on point![8]

I want to stress that we had our data for three weeks before going

---

8   Fred Imbert, "US economy grows by 3.2% in the first quarter, topping expectations," CNBC, April 26, 2019, https://www.cnbc.com/2019/04/26/gdp -q1-2019-first-read.html.

public with it. Additionally, and more importantly, our data provided insight into the future, based on current sentiment. The Coupa BSI has since been cited in *Fortune's* Quarterly Investment Guide as one of the top economic indicators.

Given the massive amount of data we have, we looked at various variables and back-tested them to see if there were correlations between what we had seen in the past two and a half years and how the economy had actually performed.

We looked at nearly everything you can think of. For example, goods and services bought. The problem with that is that data can get misleading quickly. If you buy two 12-ounce bottles of something and someone else buys one 24-ounce bottle, is that equivalent? Is the first company buying two products and the second company buying only one? The answer to both questions is yes, of course, but how can you display the information accurately? You have all kinds of data quality problems if you use a measure like that.

Another factor we looked at was inventory on hand, but that also proved difficult to correlate because sometimes the amount of inventory simply depended on how much space a company had to store it. The fact that they had no place to keep it sometimes was the reason that they didn't keep much stock on hand, not the fact that they were worried about the economy and concerned that they were going to get stuck with goods they could not sell.

But with the three factors we are using, there was a statistically sound correlation. When we back-tested them, it predicted how the economy had actually played out since 2016. With these three factors—how much we are spending, how quickly we are approving spend, and whether things are getting rejected along the way—we get much more visibility into the future.

The implications of having this data are clear. If you notice that your peers are spending aggressively, you might decide to increase your spending as well to keep up.

If I am a CEO of a company that sells to industries that seem to be bearish, I might focus my sales and marketing efforts on other industries that seem to be bullish. If I sell boxes, for example, I could sell boxes to nearly everyone. But I obviously want to sell the most I can. If I notice retailers are far more bullish than other sectors, I might focus more of my sales efforts on them and decrease my marketing in segments that are not as optimistic.

Conversely, if I am in the box business and I notice through the leading indicators that sales are going to be bad across the board, I might want to change my product mix. I might make fewer boxes and shift into making paper and start targeting financial services companies and law firms—places that don't tend to buy boxes.

You see why you want to share

Remember in Chapter 4, when we talked about privacy, that we said the only reason you would want to contribute certain company data is that you would be getting more than you contribute in return?

Well, what we are talking about here proves the point.

Your contribution (of your anonymized data) is not a big one—it doesn't take much effort, and you are not disclosing anything proprietary—but your potential gain is huge. You are getting back information that could improve your company dramatically—possibly pointing you to different strategies and tactics (see Chapter 5)—and you have the potential benefit of gaining economies of scale by joining with others to buy more cheaply the goods and services you are already using.

Now the pushback to this could be: "Obviously, Community Intelligence can improve my company, but it will probably help underperforming companies the most. If I am running a good company, why do I want to improve my competition? Sure, I'll gain a bit, but by definition they will gain more, making them a greater threat to me."

I understand the comment, but I think it misses the point. Sure, you may be running a great organization today, but your investors and everybody involved with your company are valuing your company based on its ability to do something in the future, not maintain it where it is, as we discussed in Chapter 5. So unless you're on top of what's happening at this moment and have visibility into what may happen tomorrow, you risk trending downward. That's what happens in every industry. Those that get complacent are the ones that get knocked out.

So, again you can see why having Community Intelligence is so valuable. In a world that literally gets more competitive every day, you will know where to spend your resources. You'll have visibility into what the future is going to look like and be able to be proactive instead of reactive.

OPERATIONAL EFFICIENCY

Community Intelligence should create greater industry-wide operational efficiency. Why? For one thing, each company will spend less time on needless replicated research. That's when different companies do the same research. Instead, the research and data sets will be shared across the industry. Individual companies won't have to do it.

There also will be greater collaboration in supply chains. This is an important point. With the sharing of data, people will have better insights into markets, such as which ones to enter, and they will know what their distinct value propositions are in each particular market they enter.

Not only would best practices spread more quickly, but Community Intelligence would help companies identify more quickly what they do well and allow them to focus on their core competencies while allowing others to find their differentiated core competencies.

The puzzle pieces would fit more neatly in an industry. That's the visual I have. The pieces (companies, in my metaphor) would fit rather than overlapping and forcing customers to figure out who's who and what's what. That would obviously benefit consumers. And from a company's perspective, why would I want to go where everybody else is when the data is presenting an opportunity somewhere else?

There is another advantage. This new way of doing business ought to lead to a lower likelihood of collusive practices because we will have greater visibility into industry dynamics as a whole.

Think about it. Where does collusion happen? In the dark. It happens in smoke-filled rooms where a few people get together and say, "We could screw a lot of people if we band together and keep prices high." Oil is a perfect example of that. OPEC is holding everyone hostage by price fixing.

COULD ACCESSING TOO MUCH DATA SLOW THINGS DOWN?

Is there any concern that the use of industry data will cause an industry as a whole to move too slowly? After all, it is possible that companies will wait until they have a firm grasp of what all the numbers mean before they decide to act. Could that be a downside?

No. In fact, I think exactly the opposite is the case. Having access to the data should allow companies to move more quickly. They won't have to wait another quarter to get a report. They'll have leading indicators of what might happen right there in front of them. So they'll be more inclined to act quicker with confidence and competence.

WELCOME TO THE FUTURE: WHAT'S IN IT FOR YOUR INDUSTRY EDITION

OPERATING FASTER AND MORE EFFICIENTLY TO PRODUCE GREATER RESULTS

To bring everything we just talked about in this chapter to life, let's imagine a Q+A interview with the fictional William J. Baker, professor of competitive strategy at the equally fictional (although extremely prestigious) Boston Bay University School of Business, that appears in *The Wall Street Journal* five years from now.

Professor Baker has just completed what has been described as a "groundbreaking" study of how cross-company data sharing, what we call Community Intelligence, has been changing competitive dynamics across virtually every industry you can think of over the last five years. And as you will see in the interview, he touches on how Community Intelligence transforms what happens in the four critical components for every business: **Customers**, **Suppliers**, **Employees**, and **Finances**.

Q. For those people who did not read your study, what was the most important takeaway?

At the highest level, we found that companies that leverage centralized stores of real-time data from members of their community in making strategic decisions, as well as the tactical ones in daily operations, far exceed their competitors in virtually every industry.

Q. While it would be fun to talk about every industry in depth, for the sake of simplicity, why don't we discuss just one in the rest of the questions. Let's use retail so everyone can relate.

That's fine. I can assure you that the findings are consistent no matter what industry you wish to consider.

Q. Great. So, the macro-conclusion is that companies that engaged in what we commonly call Community Intelligence outperform the competition in nearly every metric. If you can, talk about why that is true in the four areas that affect every business: customers, suppliers, employees, and finances.

Let's start with **customers**. By deeply understanding in real time what customers want, their desires, their motivations, and what they are willing to spend money on, and also understanding in real time what the trends are and are likely to be in the marketplace, forward-thinking, engaged retail fashion industry leaders have been able to present the right products at the right place at the right time to help win a greater share of wallet while, at the same time, building long-lasting, deep relationships with their existing customer base. And all these factors, of course, help them attract new customers as well.

Q. All these good things are possible because the best retailers are seeing everything you just talked about sooner than everybody else?

They're seeing it sooner because they're seeing it in real time; that's the first concept. The second is they are leveraging anonymized community data from others within their industry. They are seizing on factors that the data shows will help them, the factors that make them unique.

Q. So, where do *suppliers* fit in in all this?

The retailers that were able to grab the greatest customer wallet share were the ones that were able to get to market fastest with the products customers wanted: products that were personalized precisely for them. Getting that right required the retailers to have full visibility into both their supply base and chain, not only to obtain the quickest speed to market but also to nail the quality required, getting the best prices and avoiding any risk (such as the suppliers who might miss delivery times or even go bankrupt). Risky suppliers lead to unhappy customers. Community Intelligence helped companies avoid dealing with risky suppliers.

Q. How?

Community Intelligence allowed companies to assess in real time which would be the best suppliers that would allow them to move quickly and buy the highest quality at the lowest cost and lowest risk. Knowing that data let the retailers uphold the margin requirements, making them more operationally fit to succeed and ensuring that they could be around for the long haul. It is a very powerful tool.

Q. That's clear. But companies don't do anything. **Employees** within companies do. How did Community Intelligence help employees?

The easiest way to put it is that they could leverage what they did best. It freed them from doing rote tasks while at the same time

continued

presenting them with prescriptive advice about how to best optimize their creativity or whatever their best skills were.

Q. But wait. If Community Intelligence is giving this advantage to employees at Ralph Lauren and also to its competitors like Burberry, where is the competitive advantage for either Ralph Lauren or the employees at Burberry or at any other retailer? Isn't it just keeping the playing field level?

No. Community Intelligence allowed the companies to leverage their core competencies. Not every retailer is best at everything. Some lead with creativity and design, where others have core competencies around manufacturing and distribution. Community Intelligence allows every company, and employee within those companies, to better focus on what they do best. They could seize on the information that made their strengths stronger. It allowed them to be more operationally fit, which is different for every company.

Q. Okay, we are *The Wall Street Journal*. Let's talk about **finances**. What's the financial advantage, no matter what industry you are in, of employing Community Intelligence?

That's easy. As a result of everything we talked about, Community Intelligence allowed retailers in our example—and all companies, as we saw in our study—to operate more efficiently at greater speed with fewer people, people who were freed from rote tasks that added little or no value. That allowed companies to both increase their margins and gain greater market share.

SECTION III

Going Forward

Chapter 8

WHAT THE FUTURE ALREADY LOOKS LIKE

Up until now, we have been talking about the power of Community Intelligence in the future tense. How we *will* be able to take in all of the data and information from members of an industry and sort through it to find patterns—such as who the best suppliers are or in which areas your company is spending dramatically more than its peers—and how we *will* be able to run our business better using prescriptions. ("Consider immediately ending your arrangements with Supplier X and Supplier Y. Supplier X has a history of overcharging and double billing; Supplier Y's rate of on-time deliveries is suspect, according to the Community Intelligence.")

The takeaway message has been that we will become smarter together over time *in the future.*

But in many places the future is already here.

To effectively highlight what is already happening today, we will continue using the area of business spending as our domain of choice to highlight concepts. But it should be noted that the same underlying concepts can be applied equally to a host of other domains, such as human capital management and customer relationship management.

In the next few pages, I want to show you how various organizations, both businesses and nonprofits, have already employed Community Intelligence to operate more efficiently—saving substantial sums—and improved dramatically in the process.

Specifically, you will see how these organizations used Community Intelligence to cut costs, take advantage of early payer discounts, improve their supplier community interactions, and in general, operate more effectively.

Consider these to be snapshots from a future that is already here, based on experiences witnessed in the Coupa community. (All the examples are real, with most names disguised for anonymity.)

SETTING THE STANDARD

Let me state the obvious as we begin talking about Scheherazade!, our disguised name for one of the leaders in developing audio, imaging, and special effects for movies and computer games: *Knowing exactly where you stand is always better than relying on rumors, guessing, and conjecture.*

But when it came to knowing how much Scheherazade! was spending on management-consulting services, it was pretty much conjecture.

Facts are always better than opinions.

That was a problem. Scheherazade! was state of the art when it came to technology. My favorite fact about them may be that the company has received 11 Academy Awards and 19 Emmy Awards (so far) for their contributions to cinema and television.

> *"Scheherazade! had considerable redundancy across a large number of management-consultant suppliers. With Community Intelligence, Coupa gave me the supporting information that I needed to build an internal business case and prioritize sourcing opportunities."*
> *–Susan D. Davis, Senior Manager, Corporate Procurement, Scheherazade!*

But the organization was nowhere as impressive when it came to tracking its management-consulting spending.

One of Scheherazade!'s top priorities was to manage its costs more strategically, and according to the company's rumor mill, that wasn't happening when it came to the company's management-consulting expenses, primarily because each business unit had previously been responsible for its own supplier relationships.

Scheherazade!'s finance team had heard anecdotes about the proliferation of management consultants across the business, but they didn't have a clear idea of how much of a problem it was, or how costly.

Using Community Intelligence, Scheherazade! was able to directly compare its spending on management-consulting services against its industry peers, and what senior managers found proved all the rumors to be true.

Specifically:

- Scheherazade! discovered that 40 percent of the invoices being submitted were for management-consulting services, which was 18 times greater than the industry average.

- They had three times as many consultants as was typical for a company its size in the industry, and as Susan D. Davis, the company's senior manager for corporate procurement, pointed out: Scheherazade! had "considerable redundancy across a larger number of those suppliers."

Community Intelligence prescribed that Scheherazade! consolidate the number of management consultants it used and consider suppliers with whom others in the community were having strong results.

Armed with that information, Davis and her team built a case to prioritize sourcing opportunities when it came to management consulting firms. Consolidation of spending among fewer consultants is now underway with steady progress toward the goals of both reducing costs and improving profitability.

DEALING WITH FRAUD

The Memorial University Medical Center (they asked us to disguise their name) is a huge medical complex that includes University Health Care and University Children's Health.

Memorial University is consistently ranked as one of the best hospitals in the United States and serves as a teaching hospital for the university's school of medicine, one of the nation's best.

Established more than 150 years ago, Memorial University has

$4.5 billion in operating revenue and is one of the top designated comprehensive care centers, which means it allows cutting-edge science to flourish alongside clinical studies and treatment.

The medical center also had a problem that it was unaware of, before it began drawing on the power of Community Intelligence.

Like many teaching hospitals, Memorial University would outsource many of the services it needed, such as the ability to share patient images—X-rays, CAT scans, MRIs, and the like. The sharing allowed physicians who were part of the medical center's network to see the results of tests that had already been done. (The alternative? Repeating the tests, which would be a waste of both time and money for all involved.)

Memorial University had a long-standing relationship with a supplier who was handling about half of the image sharing, system-wide, and the medical center believed everything was fine until it noticed that members of the community—other large health-care providers, in this case—constantly rated the supplier poorly. The other hospitals reported that they were rejecting the supplier's invoices at an abnormally high rate (one in four invoices were being kicked back, instead of the average 2.5 percent).

In other words, this supplier, when compared to others, was 10 times more likely to have something wrong with its invoices—and wrong could mean anything from charging too much to double billing.

"This was the first time I saw that kind of information," said Memorial University's controller, who immediately set out to investigate if there were problems with the supplier's billing of his hospital system. There were.

In addition to overcharging on a regular basis, the supplier was sending multiple invoices for services it had not provided. Memorial

University immediately suspended working with the supplier and is in the process of clawing back close to $8 million in payments that were made for work that was either not done or had already been paid for, and its investigation is ongoing.

Perhaps my favorite part of the story is that after Memorial University switched suppliers, not only did the problems with invoices fall to well within the normal range, but the university system ended up saving 15 percent overall on its imaging bills. Its new supplier was not only better but also less expensive.

CONSOLIDATE SUPPLIERS, SAVE MONEY

With 10,000 employees and more than $4.8 billion in revenues, Williamson (we have anonymized them a bit at their request) is a global research and consulting firm devoted to creating manufacturing breakthroughs and process improvements for the auto, truck, and transportation industries. The firm works with every one of the world's top 25 transportation companies, and its sales and earnings have grown consistently since its founding generations ago.

But like every other new or established company, Williamson was interested in cutting costs. The challenge it found, when it made the commitment to do so, was where to start. So the company turned to the power of Community Intelligence to find out.

When it looked at its spending compared to that of its industry peers, Williamson saw that its restaurant and catering costs were out of whack. Hosting those big transportation clients was a huge part of its selling effort, as it was for everyone targeting this market. (It also represented about 10 percent of the invoices Williamson was processing.) But the numbers revealed that Williamson was spending about 6 percent more than the rest of the industry in this category and had 13 times as many suppliers.

Clearly, here was an opportunity. If the company could reduce the number of suppliers, it probably could get a volume discount from the remaining ones it decided to use. But how to determine which suppliers were the best to keep and which ones could be jettisoned without harm?

Again, Community Intelligence came through. Williamson's peers had rated each of the 13 suppliers Williamson used. The company winnowed its list of 13 down to 5 by concentrating on those with "excellent" or "very good" ratings. By consolidating its spending, Williamson was able to get the volume discounts it wanted. Expenses in the category were reduced by more than 10 percent in the following year.

EARLY PAYMENT DISCOUNTS

See if this sounds familiar: As your company has grown over time, systems have evolved in an ad hoc manner, following the rules of the people who designed them (as opposed to the rules governing common sense or organizational needs).

Or maybe similar systems have been mashed together following acquisitions.

In either case, things internally don't work as well as they could.

That was the situation at Global Bank, our disguised name for one of the world's largest financial institutions with well over $25 billion in revenue. It was handling invoices using many manual processes and third-party integrations and, as a result, was taking 10 days to approve an invoice, 10 times longer than its best-in-class peers, as shown to the bank via Community Intelligence.

Even worse, those slow processing times were keeping Global Bank from taking advantage of the early payment discounts many of its vendors offered.

Drawing on the power of Community Intelligence, Global Bank realized the problem was even worse than it thought. Its slow invoice-processing times were happening despite the fact that 85 percent of what the bank was buying was preapproved, a percentage that was almost 30 percent higher than similar best-in-class financial services companies.

Armed with this information, Global Bank decided to completely overhaul its underlying invoice-management processes, in many cases sending payment with orders and taking full advantage of early payment discounts negotiated with suppliers. One clearly measurable outcome is that it was able to cut its total company expenses by almost a full 1 percent, which in its case meant a savings of tens of millions of dollars annually.

OPERATING MORE EFFICIENTLY TO SERVE A VITAL MISSION

In 1941, just before the United States entered World War II, "President Franklin D. Roosevelt sought to unite several service associations into one organization to lift the morale of our military and nourish support on the home front." This is the way the United Service Organizations, better known as the USO, begins when describing its history. Parts of the service associations—the Salvation Army, Young Men's Christian Association, Young Women's Christian Association, National Catholic Community Services, National Travelers Aid Association, and the National Jewish Welfare Board—combined to both then and now "support our nation's military and their families."

Today there are more than 230 USO locations, supporting every continent and "operated by staff and volunteers whose goals are to match our service members' vigilance, and provide best-in-class service to those who sacrifice so much for America."

The USO is not part of the federal government. A congressionally chartered, private organization, "the USO relies on the generosity of individuals, organizations and corporations to support its activities," and that means, by definition, that every penny and dollar is held accountable.

> *"Community Intelligence gives us the visibility to identify improvement opportunities that we don't see anywhere else." –Rick Quaintance, Senior Director of Procurement and Contract Management, USO*

As a nonprofit that delivers goods and services to the troops, how quickly and efficiently it processes spending requests directly impacts how quickly those goods and services are delivered to our troops. Invoice-processing time was a metric that the USO was keen to reduce, yet not only didn't it have an efficient, automated way to handle invoice processing, but it also had no way of knowing what excellence looked like.

By using Community Intelligence prescriptions, the USO learned what best-in-class cycle times looked like for similar-sized nonprofits: one day for invoice processing, as it turned out.

Knowing a goal of one day was something achievable, the USO started working to reduce its cycle time, which was averaging between four and seven days. Within a matter of weeks, they were able to reduce invoice-processing time to 1.78 days by redesigning workflows and leveraging real-time end-user Community Intelligence prescriptions to help their teams move quicker and focus on what mattered for the organization.

IDENTIFYING RISKY SUPPLIERS

Founded some 70 years ago, the Leukemia & Lymphoma Society (LLS) is a nonprofit organization that is the world's largest voluntary health organization dedicated to fighting blood cancer. It has 56 chapters throughout the United States and five in Canada.

LLS has invested more than $1.3 billion in research and is a leader in advancing breakthroughs in immunotherapy, genomics, and personalized medicine.

As the organization says on its website:

"Beating Cancer is in our Blood.

"Cancer is a heck of an opponent.

"It's a bully. But we are not afraid of a fight.

"It's elusive. But our focus never fades.

"It's deadly. But we are known cancer killers.

"Since 1949, we have pioneered groundbreaking research that leads us to believe we will find the cures for cancer in our blood. We were born to defeat this opponent."

As a nonprofit that relies heavily on donations, LLS's reputation is paramount. Knowing where donor money is being spent, and with whom, is a big responsibility, one that falls completely within the purview of its finance and procurement departments.

"Now I have real-time information to monitor key suppliers, which allows us to rest easy while focusing on high-value activities." – JR Miller, CFO of LLS

Part of that responsibility is identifying risky suppliers, because donors want to know that LLS is treating their money with the utmost care and responsibility.

"For LLS, reputation is a key risk," says LLS's chief financial officer, JR Miller. "If we don't have a solid reputation, donors don't want to give us dollars. So when we're looking at our suppliers, we can't let a risky situation develop. We have to nip it in the bud before it grows into something much bigger and could impact our ability to fundraise and ultimately fund our mission."

And yet, LLS still had to contend with the limited resources of a nonprofit, which previously meant staying vigilant required a lot of manual effort from individuals on the finance team, who also bore other essential responsibilities. But once LLS began to use Community Intelligence, that burden eased tremendously.

Looking at Community Intelligence data, LLS was able to identify potentially risky suppliers that had been flagged by the system. This made it easier for the team to investigate situations and determine whether or not the suppliers truly presented a risk.

"Prior to having Community Intelligence information, we would only know about problems either when we'd see something in the newspaper or something came to light from another source," Miller explains. "But at that point, it could be too late. So we needed something like Community Intelligence to give us early indicators that something may be going off the rails with a particular supplier that we needed to address sooner than later.

"Looking at how a supplier is transacting with the rest of the community with measurable behavioral data, like rejected invoice rates and pricing consistency, helps us rest easy," Miller adds. "And having a tool that's able to bring all this information together and provide us with a holistic picture of a supplier, giving us the ability to say, 'Okay. We might've detected a financial risk or a litigation risk that we need to understand so that we can decide whether we want to continue doing business with that supplier or work with them to help us lower that risk.'"

What made Community Intelligence especially helpful as a tool was the prescriptive nature of it. The system identified potential alternatives in each of the flagged cases, should the LLS team decide to switch suppliers.

JUST GETTING STARTED

The previous cases in this chapter showed how the power of Community Intelligence could be applied in various specific instances: to catch fraud, consolidate suppliers, obtain early payment discounts, and the like.

> *Start small, if you have to, but start!*

But what if you don't know where to start when it comes to using all of this information that is now available?

That was the situation that a European national museum, one with an international reputation, found itself in. It had no real visibility into what it was spending and with whom. Sure, it knew what the overall expenses were, because each department was keeping track, but it had no idea how well it was doing when compared to its peers.

The museum decided to find out by looking at the numbers compiled by the community. The results would give it a place to begin to improve.

The museum started small. It had a general sense that most invoices were submitted manually but did not have the exact number.

It turned out that only 25 percent of invoices were being handled electronically, far below the industry average, and that the museum was aiming too low in trying to improve their systems. It set a goal of getting seven out of ten invoices processed electronically. Best-in-class institutions were handling 76 percent of them that way.

With the numbers in front of them, the museum set off to improve procedures across the organization.

For every organization and company that we just talked about, the future is already here.

Chapter 9

PULLING IT ALL TOGETHER

S o, let's pull it all together.

The big takeaways from the opening chapters were that while the ideas of community and benefiting from what the community knows have been around as long as there have been communities, our ability to access that knowledge has changed dramatically only relatively recently.

Today, we're able to collect data nonintrusively from a huge number of contributors in real time, then leverage that data for our benefit, also in real time. That simply wasn't possible before we had the systems and technology to do it. Now we do, and we can use the data to create personalized prescriptions to help our organizations compete more effectively and allow us to do our jobs better.

Why are prescriptions so important? Because—

- They leverage the power of a constantly growing community data set.

- They contextualize the data for you.

- They provide insights into your own unique (current) situation.

- They are instantly actionable ("Consider doing business with Supplier X instead of Supplier Y").

Of course, you don't have to follow the prescriptions. You remain the ultimate decision maker. But the information is something you should want to consider since it is objective, fact-based, and coming from your peers.

> *Until recently, we didn't have the systems and technology that allowed us to collect Community Intelligence, aggregate it, and personalize it in real time so that every member of the community could benefit. We do now.*

I have argued that this change is revolutionary, and it is. We now have the ability to operate at almost the speed of thought. Let's return to the Waze analogy that I used earlier in the book to explain what I mean.

You're driving along and traffic suddenly stops. There is a huge backup caused by an accident, and Waze immediately gives you a potential new route to follow. Community Intelligence does exactly the same thing. Those who have access to it will have a huge competitive advantage over those that don't. They will be able to move faster with better community-powered intelligence.

And that was another key takeaway. Hypercompetition will put every company in a situation where each individual component of value will be a competitive battleground. Community Intelligence can provide a unique advantage in that kind of environment by being able to offer the most differentiated, and the timeliest, insights.

In addition to helping us be competitively best positioned, Community Intelligence can help us fully distill how to deliver the most value at the right place and time to get the most economic benefit from our customer relationships.

So in the three waves of business that we talked about, we go from simply offering a product (Wave 1), to providing Value-as-a-Service (Wave 2), to offering exponential value, thanks to Community Intelligence (Wave 3).

It is easy to understand why things are evolving this way. Think about the world of products, for example. Anything that has a physicality, a material body, to it is getting more and more commoditized through robotics, cheaper sourcing, and the fact that pricing is becoming virtually transparent.

So, the real battleground is in the way those products are delivered through differentiated value. That's how we have moved from providing greater value in products—cars—to greater Value-as-a-Service—Uber and Lyft. You simply pay a fee for getting the value of being transported from point A to point B (Transportation-as-a-Service) in whatever value class you desire.

In the next phase, Wave 3, that service will become even more customized for you, drawing on both your preferences and powered by insights from a growing community of travelers. Not only will the cars be self-driving, and not only will your preferences be known, but based on insights collected from all travelers and current travel patterns, your entire travel experience will be fully interoperable with all other key data sources so it can be fully optimized from start to finish along every possible variable of comfort, price, schedule, safety, technical compatibility, and class level. Most importantly, the information technology (powered by Community Intelligence) will do it all. You will only have to make yourself available for the trip.

WHERE DO YOU BEGIN?

We said in Chapter 3 that there are three components of community power:

1. Data and intelligence
2. Information sharing
3. Collaboration and pooling of power

It is easy to see why these three elements are important. Everything starts with data and distilling something of value from it. But that data is only valuable when it is shared with the right people so they can do something with it. Once they're empowered with information, they have the opportunity to do powerful actions, like gaining insights or pooling their power (e.g., group purchasing).

ADDRESSING PRIVACY

As we said in Chapter 4, you don't have to share anything you don't want to. It's your information. Period. And you are certainly not going to share anything proprietary or anything that could put you at a disadvantage, and you are not going to want that information sold, unless you are profiting from it.

What follows is that you are only going to share your information if you can get intelligence in return that is greater than what you are giving, otherwise you don't have any incentive to contribute.

Then you need to know that the data is going to be sanitized, anonymized, and normalized. You'll want to know that it can't be attributed to you, unless you want it to be.

COMPANY VALUE: SEEING THE FUTURE TODAY

Why you want to contribute to Community Intelligence is simple: You want to get as much current information as you can in order to predict the future more accurately.

The value of your organization is dependent on its trajectory into the future. So, the more you can get a competitive edge about what might happen, the faster you will be able to act and position your organization for the world ahead. That is what all of your stakeholders, from investors to employees, want to see. You and your company are always being evaluated on what you will do in the future, as you build on the past.

When properly applied, Community Intelligence will help your company—

- Improve strategy, informing where and how to compete

- Identify which talent pools to target

- Target your sales prospects more effectively

- Buy more efficiently, at lower costs, and with minimal risks

- Prescribe thoughtful operational guardrails across all areas of your business . . .
- And so much more in so many places within your—or any—company

EMPLOYEE VALUE: FROM TACTICAL TO STRATEGIC

For employees, the subject of our conversation in Chapter 6, the benefits are equally pronounced. As someone who works for an organization that employs Community Intelligence, you will be able to up your game. Much work today involves data collection, aggregation, and dissemination. By having that industry-wide data compiled and presented to you in a way that helps you do your job better, you are freed from doing the rote work of collecting and sorting it. That means you can spend your time thinking about the data, balancing options, and deciding whether to take the prescriptions offered.

You will have better, more complete data, not only about your company but about your entire industry. That additional information can help you come up with additional insights. And you will get all of that information in a timelier fashion, allowing you to make better decisions.

In short, you will be moving from tactical to strategic.

INDUSTRY IMPACT: PEOPLE, PROCESS, AND TECHNOLOGY

Given everything we have talked about, you can see how your entire industry could change. Community Intelligence deals with leading indicators as opposed to trailing ones, which will allow all organizations to move faster based on far better information.

People will become even more important. While it is certainly true that the insights you will be receiving will be invaluable, it will be up to you to figure out what they mean. The good news? You will have more time to figure it out, because, as we discussed, the rote and routine portions of your job will be gone. The data will be coming from the community. And almost all of the routine parts of your job will have been turned over to technology.

But it will require thoughtful and focused people to take their game to the next level to leverage these insights for driving meaningful and timely action. These people will reshape entire industries.

Process. You will need to alter the way data and information flow through your organization. Not only will you contribute your information to the community, but you will also need to ensure that the insights you get in return go to the right people to effect meaningful change. Since that information will be coming in virtually in real time, you will need to simplify your organizational structure so that the information can flow both freely and quickly. Entire industries will be reshaped based on how quickly industry participants reorganize themselves in real time.

Technology. Given points one and two, the technology you use will become even more important since it will have to enable both your people and your processes with agility and simplicity. Entire industries will be reshaped based on which technology solutions are adopted and how they are applied to business problems, based on the intelligence provided by the community.

"

Clever, resourceful people will use Community Intelligence to transform their jobs, organizations, and even their industries.

"

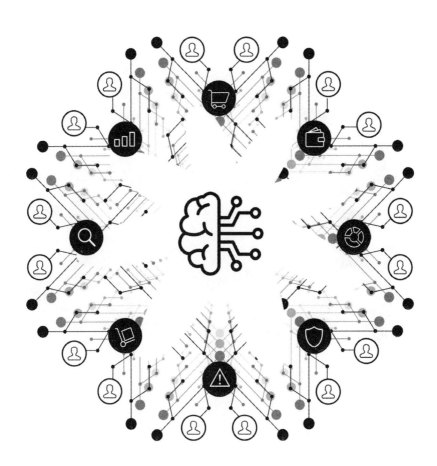

Chapter 10

TAKING COMMUNITY INTELLIGENCE TO THE EXTREME: DATE NIGHT IN 2025

To understand how the power of Community Intelligence could play out in both your personal and professional life, let's pick a time in the near future, the year 2025, and see how part of your Saturday might play out.

You start your afternoon with a workout class, in your home, in anticipation of a dinner date with your partner that evening. You hop on your cardio machine, where an instructor appears through a built-in, web-enabled screen. An optimal class is prescribed for you from a robust library of available options. The prescription takes into account all your personal desires and leverages all your accessible personal shareable data:

- Your range of music preferences

- Your list of favorite instructors

- Your next scheduled activity on your daily calendar, and accounting for historical shower times

The prescription also takes into account Community Intelligence. To render the most optimal prescription for which class you should take, it considers—

- Your optimal sustainable healthy weight relative to your current weight, which is tracked via your connected personal bathroom scale and the average calorie burn by those who have taken the class before in your age range, sex, and cardiovascular performance level

- The classes enjoyed most by those in a similar context of an evening workout ahead of a date night, based on the anonymized schedules of all community members in a similar peer group

- The likely short-term metabolic boost you'll need to sustain optimal calorie burn ahead of your scheduled dinner, factoring in your personal metabolism and the common meals enjoyed by those like you at the restaurant you are about to go to that night

You begin your 37-minute, high-intensity workout with Julie, one of your favorite instructors because of the intense workout and the fact that she's great at motivating you. You sweat through your workout while listening to Julie shout instructions over some of your favorite songs, which are dynamically being curated based on your performance during the workout because they are more likely to inspire you to get to your optimal calorie burn and desired metabolic boost.

Dinner is at a restaurant in your neighborhood, so you and your partner decide to walk (based on a suggestion that presents itself on your phone), now knowing that you will have precisely the right amount of time to arrive based on your reservation time, historical strolling pace, and current weather conditions. Upon being seated, you're handed an iPad containing the menu. On the first page are five suggestions selected just for you. All have ruled out anything you are allergic to, account for the things you have previously ordered to avoid duplicating anything you've had to eat in the last 48 hours, and are within the caloric parameters you've set and are able to burn off based on your recent workout performance and optimal health levels. The suggestions also take into account the meals you are most likely to enjoy, based on your personal recorded history of optimally digestible ingredients, and the meals that were enjoyed at this particular restaurant recently by those with your general preferences, style, and tastes.

Dinner is lovely, and you decide to go see a film. "Take us to the movies," you say into your watch, and a self-driving car is instantly summoned. It is, of course, the kind (model, style) that you like, based on your preferences, and the one with the highest likelihood of getting you to the right movie on time, based on traffic patterns, range of movie options you typically want to choose from, your historical movie choice decision times, and the current available inventory of theater seating that meets your historical range of preferences.

Once in the car, two film suggestions pop up on your phone. The first is for a thriller, your typical choice when you and your partner go out to a theater, according to your film-going history, and recommended because it received a 93 percent approval rating by couples in your peer group. The other option is a romantic comedy, typically your second choice, that just opened, and it is recommended for consideration in part based on the number of smiles recorded through facial recognition of those in your peer group.

You select your movie, arrive just in time, take your seats, and enjoy the show, all while optimally digesting, unreservedly smiling, and fully enjoying your companionship and shared experience.

Community Intelligence has optimized every aspect of your date night.

FACT, NOT FICTION

Twenty years ago, or maybe even 10 years ago, all of this would have struck people as both Big Brother–like and impossible. Today, I think most of us will agree that it is simply the logical evolution of the way things are going. Sure, it may not happen exactly as envisioned, but it will likely be pretty close. Already today, Amazon, Netflix, and countless other businesses are making increasingly targeted recommendations for you based on your past behavior and the behaviors of people like you.

Is it Big Brother–like? Well, no. You still ultimately make the final decision. You didn't need to go to either of those movies, for example. You didn't have to eat that meal. You didn't have to take that workout. Just like in the business situations we talked about, you retain ultimate control of the decision-making process, but Community Intelligence gives you more and better choices in less time.

That's good in your personal life.

And it is good in your professional life as well.

That's why you may want to join the Community Intelligence Revolution.

A (PURCHASING) REVOLUTION WITHIN THE REVOLUTION

Purchasing anything for your company should work the way it does when you buy something for yourself. Businesses should demand no less.

Do you know anyone—a friend, relative, or colleague—who prides themselves on being a naïve shopper, one who doesn't look to get the absolute best deal and the exact outcomes they want?

Of course you don't.

We all want the best value. (There is a reason they call the long-running television game show *The Price Is Right* and not *You Paid Too Much*.)

So why don't we demand the same thing in business, making it extremely easy to get exactly what we want when we want it in the process?

I think it's time we should.

Let me give you a bit of background and context for why I think that time has come.

When I was growing up, shoppers didn't have much power. Retailers set a price for an item, and you either bought it or you didn't. Remember MSRP pricing? The seller's attitude was take it or leave it. Finding out if there was a better deal took a lot of work. You had to go from store to store or spend a long time on hold as you called around to try to find a lower price or better terms (free shipping, faster delivery). The internet as we know it didn't exist then.

Today, when you and I are doing our holiday shopping, or any purchasing for that matter, all that information is available with a click or a tap, and there are even apps that will search for the lowest possible price on the things we want. Buyers now have more information than sellers. The power has shifted, and it is easy for every shopper to be smart.

> *The power has shifted from the sellers to the buyers, and it will never shift back. As information becomes more and more transparent, those with the money to spend will have more and more power.*

We need to make business shopping (i.e., buying everything from hardware to software to complex services) this simple—and clearly it isn't.

Let's take a comparative example to make the point.

Recently, I wanted to buy my eldest son some Bluetooth headphones. When I searched the places that sell them online, I was offered the following information:

- The various headphones available and how much
  they cost
- How the ones I was considering compared to others
  out there
- The rating of each vendor selling those particular
  headphones

I could also see what other shoppers thought:

- How many people bought each brand (is it a best
  seller in its particular category?)
- How much the people who purchased them liked
  them (what do the reviews say?)
- What else people found necessary to buy along with
  the headphones (a water-resistant cell phone armband
  case, etc.)

This data is far from perfect. Sure, I don't have any information on actual usage statistics from the community of users, and I
didn't have feedback from every single customer who bought the
headphones, but it was a lot better than what we have in business
purchasing.

Consider what happens if you simply want to buy 10 desks
for a new wing of your office. Odds are that your firm may have
a contract with a national supplier. Do you know if that supplier
has the best prices and fastest shipping? The quality you want? The
lowest risk of late deliveries? The lowest likelihood of overinvoic-
ing? Not without doing a lot of research and then scrambling to
find an alternative if needed. And there are at least three problems
with that.

First, companies are still largely stuck with physical or electronic catalogs. Even digitally, business buyers operate in siloed environments in which they can only visit one online catalog at a time, requiring them either to buy off of a relatively static catalog or hunt around for particular items within a given supplier site. It's a fundamentally different experience from being able to compare suppliers, goods, and services all at a glance and with prescriptions available at the touch of a button.

Second, businesses can't harness their collective power. They miss out on group buying. One of the biggest trends to come out of China's e-commerce giants is group buying, where shoppers get together and agree to buy the same product for big discounts. Businesses still don't do this much in the United States, even though, ironically, they often share the same suppliers and could benefit greatly by getting increased volume discounts, shipping discounts, and so on. Couldn't this concept be more widely applied in B2B transactions? Why are companies still not collaborating for mutual benefit? It seems obvious that they should, particularly through the use of the information technology at their fingertips.

And finally, businesses don't have access to the wisdom of the crowd. They don't know anything about the real experiences folks are having in the aggregate with suppliers. It's amazing that businesses have traditionally had limited or no detailed real-time information from peer companies in their industry about suppliers—the sellers of office furniture in this case.

That is simply not acceptable. Not having access to this kind of information is holding business buyers back. It's making them inefficient at best and putting them at a disadvantage.

We have to change this. Specifically, we need to—

- Break down the silos and aggregate the data on spending company-wide. Far too often, companies don't have a complete picture. Each department can tell you what they are spending, and on what, but total spend figures are either hard to come by or unavailable.

- Learn more about our suppliers. Which ones are the best? Who delivers the fastest, is the most reliable, and has the best service in addition to the lowest prices? Who is risky, and how can we mitigate that risk?

- Draw on the experience of other companies who buy the same sort of things we do or leverage similar services.

- In short, we need a purchasing revolution within the Community Intelligence Revolution.

Appendix II

COUPA AT WORK

We practice what we preach.

While neither this book nor this Appendix is supposed to be a commercial for Coupa, I thought it was important to spend a minute to show that our company does provide Community Intelligence to our customers.

The easiest way to understand what we do is to think of Coupa Community Intelligence, our name for the collective wisdom of our customers coupled with artificial intelligence that finds patterns in all the information that our customers provide, as Waze for business spending.

Waze, as we've talked about, has significantly improved navigation by using real-time, crowdsourced insights to prescribe the best route for drivers. Similarly, Coupa uses real-time insights from our community to prescribe the best steps to drive results in business spend management for our customers.

Specifically, we provide the following services:

Benchmarking. We can tell you how much you are spending in various categories versus your peers, and we can tailor those benchmarks to your company's goals, such as how well you are progressing toward your objective of cutting expenses by 8 percent this year, or whatever goal you are trying to achieve.

Giving you general insights. We identify places where you can save money and improve the way your organization spends by giving you recommendations based on proven community best practices to help you speed goal completion. For example, we can show you how to increase your first-time invoice match rate or ways to structure approvals to reduce cycle times.

Offering insights about your suppliers. Which ones are you spending the most money with? How does that compare to your peers? How can you maximize your spend with those suppliers to get the biggest discounts or best terms?

Finding the best suppliers. Customers can search for suppliers who meet their specific needs when it comes to quantity, quality, and price and filter for trustworthiness, the ability to ship to different regions, ratings, certifications, and more.

Identifying potential problem suppliers. We flag in real time risky suppliers (those whose credit scores have dropped, are on government watch lists, or have filed for bankruptcy) and suggest replacements, all done by leveraging our rapidly growing data set and the Community Intelligence distilled from it.

Detecting fraud—before it happens. We use community spend data to flag suspicious individuals for audit in the area of expense management. Looking at patterns across our hundreds of billions of dollars in spending patterns, we can help companies identify fraud quickly and effectively. What's missing with most fraud detection technology is that it looks at fraud in a silo. But fraud is a human behavior. Employees who commit fraud will generally not limit themselves to only one area; they will try to do it everywhere. So our platform engine scans spend data to identify potential employee-level patterns for suspicious activity. This is a radical shift in business fraud detection. We don't want to simply detect fraud after it happens. We want to control it before your money goes out the door. No more employee expense fraud.

We help customers detect supplier fraud as well—no more duplicate invoices, and much more. Coupa prescribes solutions, such as putting a risky supplier on hold while they are investigated, and suggests others you can use in the interim.

This is why I am so excited about the idea of using community data. Coupa is real proof that it works for hundreds of companies all over the world.

ACKNOWLEDGMENTS

Special thanks to the Coupa team:

John Adger

Karri Adkins

Daniel Adrian

Neeraj Advani

Nagabhushana Agasanur

Stephen Aghaulor

Massimiliano Agostinoni

Vaibhav Agrawal

Abhishek Agrawal

Anchal Agrawal

Jean Aguirre

Judy Ahadian

Mohamed Shafi
    Ahamed Haja

Sachin Aher

Kenneth Ahlquist

Nihal Ahmed

Chandrababu Ajish

Saloni Ajmera

Ara Akoubian

Julie Alben

Sreekhar Ale

Vanessa Aleksic-Brown

Benjamin Almarza

Ana Caroline Almeida

Yamila Alonso

Jose Maria Alonso Garcia

Adam Alphin

Vincent Alquier

Sal Alswafta

Ahmad Al-Ta'ani

Airiel Altemara

Marco Altieri

Jonathan Altoé

Fernando Álvarez Castro

Tiago Miguel Alves de Melo

Bharath Alwala

Suzana Amer

Isabella Amfo

David Ammerman

Nitin Amrutkar

Sudhir Anarasi

Robert Anderson

Per Andersson

Arne Andersson

Kerstin Andersson

Matthew Andrews

Jonathan Angress

Swapnil Anjikar

Brandon Ankney

Lindsay Anthony

Tatsuya Aoyama

Rucha Apte

Antonio Ardila

Elysha Armbruster

Hala Armstrong

Rohit Arolkar

Charchit Arora

Saurabh Arora

Neha Arora

Francesca Arru

Sreedhar Arudra

Hiroki Asaeda

Himanshu Ashish

David Ashton

Recep Aslan

Pouyan Assadi-Lamouki

Anureet Asthana

Jason Atkins

Jonathan Atkinson

Mounika Atmakur

Jeremy Aubert

Pierre Aubry

James Audas

Kamalakar Aukunooru

Justin Aul

Ricardo Avalos

Akash Avandhe

Jose Agustin Avila Perez

Sudhakar Awula

Preston Azubuike

Sai Baba

Tarun Babbar

Kelly Babbit

Christopher Babeu

Sneha Baby

Delia Baciu

Henry Backman

Bharathi Badeneni

Jitesh Badgujar

Tejaswini Bagade

Amit Baid

Rajat Bajpai

Danielle Baker

Heather Baker

Shrilekha Balkawade

Laxman Goud Bandi

Krati Bansal

Kristine Barats

Maurizio Baratta

James Barbour

Sukhada Bardapurkar

SK Fayaz Bari

Kristi Barker

Donald Barker

Allison Barry

Christopher Bartolo

Jay Patrick Batalla

Vamshi Batchu

Gina Bates

Brandon Bauer

Kevin Bauer

Philip Baumann

Carl Baumcratz

Sujay Bawaskar

George Baxter

David Beahm

Ronald Beardsley

Michael Beasley

Jared Bechthold

Nicole Beck

Gangadhar Bejugam

Meyer Belahcen

Dennis Belavich

Timothy Bell

Fanny Bellec

Kathleen Belotto

Farah Benkirane

Daniel Benson

Douglas Benson

Daniel Benton

Adit Berde

Daniel Beretta

Nicole Ann Bermudez

Sidney Bernstein

Forrest Berrey

Marco Berroya

Asif Bhanwadia

Nishthaa Bhardwaj

Kamal Bhargav

Neha Bharti

Shailesh Bhaskaran

Imreet Bhatia

Ekta Bhattad

Anjali Bhosale

Daniele Bianca

Valerio Bianchi

Frank Bickerle

Brian Bigger

Ramya Bikkam

Chad Billingsley

Tracy Billups

Shilpi Biswas

Chandrashekar Bittugondanahalli Narayan

Louis Bizouerne

Maria Bizova

Martin Björling

Roger Bjornstedt

Jonathan Black

Jonathan Blanton

Scott Blatnica

Signe Blum

Alexander Boehme

Kellie Bogardus

Srinivas Bogimi

Boris Bokern

Sunil Bolina

Linus Boman

Bret Bonine

Kim Bonnar White

Phillip Boone

Hanieh Borhanazad

Prakash Borkar

Boniface Botha

Kieran Brady

Michael Brady

Leonardo Brandao

Amy Brandt

Jason Braun

Louis Braun

Harvey Brauner

Maggie Breitmayer

Sara Brind

Alexis Britt

Neil Britton

Adam Bronte

Lisa Brookman

Joseph Brooks

Jonathan Browdy

Robert Brown

David Brown

Eric Brown

Benjamin Brown

James Brown

Michael Brown

Scott Brubaker

Deborah Bryant

Matthew Buckingham

Mary Buckley

Lucy Buecking

Gabriele Buffarini

Jordan Bulkoski

Emi Janela Bumanglag

Alef Burghouts

David Burke

Sean Burns

Joseph Burns

Cinthia Buske

Paul Bustin

Jeffrey Byrd

Brian Byrne

Jennifer Caffiero

Matthew Caffiero

Mathew Calabro

Susanna Calhoun

John Callan

Kelli Cameron

Gregory Campbell

Melissa Cannavino

Frank Cappel

John Carlton

Sarah Carmichael

Roberta Carus

Claudio Carvalho

Shane Casey

Kelly Casey

Callum Cashman

Guillaume Cassegrain

Trisha Cassidy

Michael Caster

Lindsay Castro

Roberto Castro Matteotti

Natalie Cedeno

Katarina Cehovski

Umut Celik

Jasneel Chaddha

Zehana Chagani

Jojo Chalissery

Sumeet Chamoli

Daniel Chan

Jimmy Chandra

Joshua Chang

Fang-Kuey Chang

Jonathan Chaplin

Elaine Chapman

Richard Chapman

Adam Charlton

Sravankumar Chatla

Shuchi Chatterjee

Vidhya Chatterjee

Geeta Chaudhari

Abdul Chaudhry

Prithviraj Chauhan

Ravindra Chebiyam

Jyothirmayudu Cheerla

Venu Chembu

Shanying Chen

Chaitanya Chennareddy Gari

Ramki Cherukuri

Jayesh Cheruli

Sean Cheung

Nikhil Chhajed

Sofia Chiavini

Viresh Chibber

Nagaraj Chincholi

Jayadev Sai Chitturi

Narasimha Rao Chityala

Govardhan Reddy Chokkannagari

Kamila Cholawska

Julianna Chomos

Tanvi Chopade

Pooja Choudhari

Amish Choudhary

Thomas Chow

Mark Christensen

Kevin Christopher-George

Kevin Chu

Peng Chuang

Alberto Ciaramella

Alan Cima

Gina Cimarelli

Terry Clark

Kevin Clark

Carl Claughton-Wallin

Jacob Clelland

Vanesa Clucas Martin

Mike Coburn

Daniele Cocco

Spencer Cohen

Durukan Colak

Brian Colditz

Craig Coleman

Patrick Collins

Jeffery Collins

Javier Conde Monteoliva

Zhong Cong

Lindsey Conn

Toon Convents

Michael Conway

Robert Cook

Gene Cook

Charles Cooke

Jeffrey Cooper

Samuel Corl

James Corner

Itamar Correia

Rob Costelloe

Mark Courser

Vadim Courtheoux

Phillip Cousins

Sabrina Covarrubias

Paul Coviello

Benjamin Cowger

Philip Cox

Connor Cox

Michael Cram

Fabrice Cransac

Joseph Critchley

Geraldine Crivelli

James Crocitto

Jeffrey Crowder

Kathleen Crowe

Niall Cryan

Roman Cueni

Adam Cumming

Harold Cuppaidge

Emma Curran

Ren Curry

Abigail Curtice

Rhonda Cusack

Timothy Cushing

Stephen Cussen

Carol Dacunto

Ashley Dale

Shruti Dalvi

Steven Daly

Maximilian Dalziel

Douglas Damico

Vi Dang

Joshua Danielson

Donald Darby

Ketan Darji

Parand Darugar

Szabina Darvasi

Tania Darzi

Mahesh Dass

Shashank Dass

Durgam Dastagiri

Mary Daubner

Mithilesh Dave

Jordan Davenport

Abigail David

Jonathan Davies

Charles Davis

Stephen Davis

Benjamin De Point

Riaan de Rouwe

Ashwin Deekonda

Rex Dela Rosa

Cassandra Delamotte

Amanda Delfino

Mark Deluca

Adena DeMonte

Umut Deniz

Ryan DePoy

Pallavi Deshmukh

Dattatray Deshmukh

Anand Deshpande

Rajasekhar Desu

Hanno Detlefsen

Roshan Devadiga

Daniel DeVall

Simon Devane

Marco Devilla

Snigdha Dharmavaram

Jyoti Dhaware

Pradhyumna Dhondi

Pankaj Dhoot

Sandeep Dhumale

Kim Dickson

Michael Dietz

Peter DiFalco

Lisa Dillon

Dan Dimerman

Vickinda Dinnel

Rama Venkata Divvi

Kathryn Doebler

Eleanore Dogan

Sai Laxman Domakonda

Johann Doman

Hunter Donovan

Brian Dorgan

Nichole Dorsey

Ryan Dotson

Kyle Dowling

Rupali Dravid

Tanya Duckworth

Michael Duddy

Mangesh Dudhal

Niall Duffy

Patrick Duffy

Emma Dugan

Fathima Rajesh Reddy
Duggimpudi

Douglas Duker

Caleb Dunithan

Hakan Duran

Timothy Durkin

Olivier Duval

Anthony DyPac

Joshua Easterly

Martin Easton

Terry Eaton

Afaaf Ebrahim

Enrique Echeverria Ayesta

Erik Edward

Luke Edwards

Ramesh Eerla

Aboozar Eghdam

Mark Eichhorn

Stefan Einecke

Emeka Ejiofor

Claes Ekstrom

Ulf Ekstrom

Pearly Emmenegger

Mark Emmenegger

Derek Ensinger

Niharika Eranki

Timothy Esplin

Victoria Esposito

Simone Esposito Fiorendo

Jose Estrada

Andriana Evangelista

Brandon Evans

Brahma Reddy Evuri

David Eyres

Caroline Fahey

Mikin Faldu

Zaki Fall

Warren Fan

Declan Fanning

Brian Farr

Kevin Farrell

Jean-David Faure

Fernanda Faustino da Silva

Jonathan Fear

Valérie Ferat

Michael Ferguson

Saverio Ferme

Sean Fernandes

Jeremy Anne Fernandez

Luis Ferreira

Sonny Fian

Andrea Fiebiger

Lucas Fiesta

Dmitri Filatov

James Filsinger

Jared Filsinger

Dawn Fink

Stefanie Fischer

Allan Fish

Maurice Fitzgerald

Michael Florin

Mary Flynn Barton

Steven Foley

Jason Fong

Todd Ford

Tyler Ford

Angus Forrester

Anthony Forster

Sebastian Forstmann

Didier Fortes

Erica Fortune

Jeffrey Foster

Phil Foti

Darren Fourie

Jonathan Frankel

Erik Frankford

Rebecca Frediani

Joseph Freitag

Steven Fremgen

Brandon Freshour

Malte Freymuth

Shaye Friedman

Michael Frieling

Pierre Frouin

Christopher Fung

James Furney

Chaitrali Gaikwad

Swapnil Gaikwad

Paresh Gajeshwar

Sridivya Galipelli

Amy Gallagher

Phil Gallant

Sharon Galler

Pavan Kumar Gampa

Dragos Ganea

Rajalakshmi Ganesan

Prerana Gangawane

Naga Mallika Garapati

Jacob Garcia

Roque Garcia

Nicholas Garcia

Carlos Garza

Anusha Gatti

Alanna Gatto

Sunil Gautam

Kevin Gay

Drew Geiman

William George

Eric German

Sameer Ghate

Arpit Ghiya

Aviroop Ghosh

Sunjit Ghosh

Avik Ghosh

Supti Ghosh

Stephen Gibbs

Sébastien Gibelli

Andrew Gibson

Gregory Gillis

Dusti Gilmore

Paul Giroux

Clair Gladstone

Shane Gleim

Robert Glenn

Rachel Glover

Daniel Godbold

Paul Goddard

Sumit Gogia

Michael Goldberg

Jan Golding

Taviti Naidu Golla

Ashley Gomez

Carlos Gomez

Javier Gonzales Castillo

Miriam Gonzalez

Robert Gonzalez

William Goodall

Sreeharsha Gopalakrishna

Priya Gopinath

Naailah Gora

Stefanie Gordish

Robert Gordon

Akshay Gore

Udayabhaskar Goriparthi

Aisling Gorman

Babasaheb Gosavi

Matthew Goshgarian

Jonathan Goss

Roger Goulart

Joshua Gould

Jayashree Govarthanarayanan

Kandharuben Govender

Sundeep Goyal

Hitesh Goyani

Benjamin Grab

Knut Inge Gram

Courtney Gribble

Anthony Grimes

Mark Grube

Ben Grudda

Udo Gruenhoff

Ashley Grush

Alexandria Guccione

Admario Guedes

Maria Gueli

Annelise Gueydan
Alison Guilbeaux
Jonathan Guip
Geetha Krishna Reddy Gujju
Mohanpreet Gujral
Surya Guntur
Rati Gupta
Aditya Gupta
Abhijeet Gupta
Anju Gupta
Nikki Gupta
Gina Gustafson
Hans Gustavson
Gregory Gustin
Jessie Guy-O'Regan
Alicia Haag
Nicholas Haddad
Peter Hader
Andria Haggard
Jerker Hagglund
Christopher Hahn
Christopher Haigy
Kaushik Halder
Megan Hall
Clayton Halvorson
Tom Ham
Matthew Hamilton
David Hamilton
Phillip Hamilton
Luke Hammond
Raja Hammoud
Susan Hans
Jesse Happel
Russell Hardie
Nitesh Hardikar
Joseph Harding
Daniel Harper
Katherine Harper
Thomas Harris
Scott Harris
yogesh Harsh
James Hartford

Michael Harvey
David Hasegawa
David Hatch
Shirish Hatwalne
Tushar Hawaldar
Andrew Hawayek
Patrick Hayes
Anjan Hazra
Michael Heeks
Rishi Hegde
Doreen Heller
Jeffrey Hellman
Jesper Hellstrom
Paul Hennessy
Nigel Henshaw
Robert Hernandez
Stephan Herrel
Daniel Hess
Eve Higgs
Trisha Himm
Stefan Himmler
William Hinkle
David Hinton
Soumya Hirakki
Didier Hivoux
Per Hjelm
Bonnie Ho
Luc Ho
Mark Hodge
Kelsey Hoffman
Owen Hoffman
Rebecca Hoffman
Oskar Holland
Virginie Hollanders
Claes Holmgren
Jessica Holt
Arati Honyal
Josiah Hopkins
Kimberly Hopman
Michael Hopwood
Markus Hornburg
Steven Horwitz

Yutaka Hosoai
Batool Hossainzadeh
Ace Howard
Michael Hsu
Kirsten Hubert
Fran Hudson
David Huebner
Erik Huerta
Elise Huggins
Stephen Hughes
Michael Huhn
Krystal Hunt
Darryl Hunt
David Hurl
Simon Hurst
Kevin Hurst
Macshuff Hussain Biabani
Carla Hussey
Mika Huuhtanen
Odera Ikenna-Obioha
Vadym Ilin
Asma Inamdar
Vitus Irudaya
Rajesh Iyer
Mandar Jabade
Andres Jacinto
Thiago Jackiw
Shayla Jackson
Paul Jackson
Terry Jacobs
Kristin Jacobsen
Utkarsh Jadhav
Santosh Jadhav
Hamno Jaff
Ritika Jain
Deepak Jain
Shoan Jain
Pallav Jakhotiya
Rohit Jalisatgi
Eva Janos
Kevin Jansz
Supriya Jaripatke

Miroslaw Jaworski

Yolanda Jeannerat

Martin Jespersen

Saravanapavan Jeyaramanan

Veena Jhawar

Chandan Jhunjhunwal

Samantha Ji

JingChao Jiang

Komal Jogal

Santhoshi Jogimohanty

Peter Johann

Celeste Johnson

Annie Johnson Graffam

TaRon Jones

Caleb Jones

David Jorgensen

Mrudula Joshi

Vishwas Joshi

Jerome Josserand

Maggie Joy

Kadri Jugandi

Fernando Juliyanto

Jayesh Juneja

Susan Jung

Brett Kaarto

Raveendranath Kadi

Prashant Kajale

Ramu Kalavendi

Aniruddha Kale

Tejashri Kale

Ashish Kale

Dinesh Kalkhundiya

Bhama Kalyan

Saraswathi Kambam

Ronney Kandah

Vijaya Kandru

Jeffrey Kane

Dennis Kanegaye

Yongdok Kang

Sooraj Kaniparambil

Sinduja Kannan

Srinivas Kannan

Kumar Kannipoti

Niraj Karhe

Priyanka Karmarkar

Sujatha Karnati

Swati Karpur

Shiva Ranjani Kasanagottu

Dhiraj Kasar

Pragya Kashyap

Durga Prasad Katari

Ganesh Kathare

Bhaskara Kattamuri

Payal Kaul

ParvezAhamad Kazi

Tamara Keller

Kevin Kelly

Adam Kelly

Jack Keogh

Ronan Kerouedan

Catherine Keveryn

Kalim Khan

Rohit Khandale

Kakada Khath

Bharati Khokle

Puneet Khushwani

Mayuresh Khuspe

Stuart Kiel

Fabian Kienle

Anne Kim

Terry Kim

Keeyoung Kim

Eddy Kim

Jason Kim

Caroline Kimble

Alena Kireeva

Mikayla Kirkpatrick

Koji Kitagaito

Sanjesh Kizhakkekara Vasu

Mattias Kjetselberg

Thomas Klein

Steven Knapp

Mark Knight

Dane Knight

Thomas Knott

Andrew Knotts

Rene Knuth

Joerg Koester

Naresh Koganti

Aneet Kohli

Anandamayee Kolipaka

Anil Kona

Srinivasarao Konakanchi

Sheshashayana Kondannagari

Uday Konduru

Mounica Koneru

Anil Koneru

Liyun Kong

Tyler Koopmans

Roger Kopfmann

Alexandra Kor

Tanmay Korlekar

Gary Korman

Dmitri Korobov

Dileep Kumar Reddy Kotha

Naresh Kotha

Srinivasa Kotha

Panagiotis Kotsonis

Nicole Kovacs

Sai Vasudha Koya

Carter Krach

Valter Kraemer

Fabian Kramer

Jayaprakash Krishnamoorthy

Aravinth Krishnasamy

Mary Anne Krzeminski

Rohan Kshatriya

Shailesh Kulkarni

Raghavendra Kulkarni

Prasanna Kulkarni

Shishir Kulkarni

Mahendra Kulkarni

Sandeep Kulkarni

Christopher Kulmatycki

Alok Kumar

Rubesh Kumar

Deepak Kumar

Ganesh Santosh Anil Kumar

Prasanna Kumar

Himica Kumar

Pravin Kumbhar

Rajender Kundhuri

John Kurfess

Venkatesh Kurma

Aldo Kurnia

Surya Pradeep Kurunella

Ratish Kurup

Mithlesh Labroo

James LaCamp

Zelina Lacanglacang

Fatima Vhey Lacanlale

Mark Lachappell

Lindsay Lacy

Kushal Ladha

James Laframboise

Bing-Chang Lai

Malika Lamali

Louise Lamb

Luke Lamberson

Dmytro Landberg

David Langenmayr

Lori LaPara

David Larsen

Claire Larsen

Andy Lau

Paul-Jason Lawrence

Patrick Lawton

Valerie Layman

Gerald Lazanis

Dung Tien Le

Derrick Leck

John Leck

Jenny Lee

Jason Lee

Thomas Lefèvre

Brian Leibforth

Jose Leiva

Milos Lekovic

Felipe Lemos Carvalhedo

Luke Leonard

Andrea Lessani-Willits

Christine Lessard

Kira Letskina

German Lettieri

Krista Letz

Casey Levine

Sean Levy

Kristi Lewandowski

Kelcie Lewis

JingJing Li

Lizhen Li

Kimberly Liang

Kristian Lieberg

Andy Lightfoot

Ariane Lindblom

Emelie Lindfelt

Janice Liner

Jeremy Linkletter

Justin Lipton

Anna Lisboa

Yiran Liu

Yang Liu

Le Liu

Mykhailo Liubarskyi

Leah Livingston

Jure Ljubicic

Jeffrey Lo

Jayde Look

Gregory Loomis

James Losole

Benny Lu

Julian Lucas

John Lucas

Michelle Luckie

Ewelina Luckiewicz

Frank Ludwig

Pawel Lukomski

Gottfried Lumpi

Maria Lund

Martin Lynch

Richard Lynk

Brenton Lyon

Jose M J

Lindsay MacLean

Vilas Madapurmath

Nikhil Madishetty

Elisabeth Magnee-Schalch

Kyle Magocs

John Maguire

Saurabh Mahajan

Supriya Mahajan

Muhammad Mahmood

Jonathan Mainella

Nessim Makhloufi

Andrew Malay

Karan Malhotra

Maruti Malladi

Sascha Mallinowski

Rachel Malzacher

Akshay Manchalwar

Elizabeth Mancini

Ruth Mancuso

Peter Mancuso

Sujay Mandal

Shatabdi Mandal

Aditya Mandavilli

Darshan Mandhane

Sandip Mandlecha

Richard Mangahas

Pooja Mangla

Thierry Mangogna

Pavithra Mani

Bharath Manicka Vasagam

Brendan Manion

Michael Manna

Venkata Manne

Florian Marchal

Gregory Mark

Daniel Mark

Priscila Marques Alves

Mauricio Marroquin

Richard Marshall

Aaron Martin

Raymond Martinelli

Juan Martinez Perez

Matthieu Martini

Christopher Martini

Sean Martyn

Paul Martyn

Pallavi Mathane

Soby Mathew

Shuchi Mathur

Mayank Mathur

Nikita Mathur

John Mattinson

Jon Mauro

Rajesh Mavideda

Mark Maxwell

Alexa May

Christopher Mayor

Dmitry Mazalov

Andrew Mazid

Kathleen Mc Intyre

Michael Mc Kay

Bram McCabe

Glynis McCabe

Mark McCarthy

Simon McCarthy

Joshua McCarty

Pamela McClure-Roman

Ian McDean

Jesse McDermott

Maggie McGoldrick

Sandy McGregor

Jacob McHenry

Aaron McIntyre

Kristian McKenzie

Kerri McManus

Derek McNeil

Ian McNelly

Michael McNulty

Vishvarup Mehta

Yatish Mehta

Rahul Mehta

Paula Meidinger

Eva-Maria Meier

Oleksandr Mekhovov

Samuel Mele

Paul Menciassi

Ashley Menezes

Rebecca Mengell

James Merrick

Timothy Merrifield

Eric Merriman

Louis Merz

Brock Metcalf

Stephanie Metcalfe

Tushar Metkar

Kent Mewhort

Stephanie Meyer

Aakash Mhankale

Marc Middlekauff

Anukthi Mijar

Keaton Miller

Craig Miller

Laurel Miller

Ian Milligan

Ralitza Minchev

Lakshmi Sailaja Miriyala

Max Mishka

Sankalp Mishra

Mihaela Mitelea

Anshul Mittal

Benjamin Mlynash

Siyandiswa Mnyanda

Nikhil Mohadikar

Sara Mohtashamipour

Wilfrido Molina Santillan

Robert Monahon

Gabrielle Monetti

Priscilla Monteiro Simoes

Curtis Moore

Sunil More

Rodrigo Morelli

Roman Moreno

David Morgenstern

Toru Mori

Victoria Morley

Rebecca Morris

Michelle Moy

Masoud Mozayeni

Vinod Kumar Yadav Mucha

Kusno Mudiarto

Jill Muellner

Avijit Mukherji

Aslam Mulani

Riyaz Mulla

Ketan Mundada

Robert Munoz

Dan Muntean

Vaishnavi Muralidhar

Jessica Murillo

Rachael Musengo

Nicholas Myers

Abigail Myers-Antiaye

Ilana Myerson

Revathi Nagainallur Murali

Sanket Naik

Miho Nakazawa

Bhanu Vignesh Nalla

Jimmy Nalls

Shreesh Namboor

Nageswara Reddy
Nandarapu

Vaibhav Nanotkar

Ankit Narang

Swati Narayane

Shrinivas Narayani

Vinay Narayanunni

Bharat Narra

Patricia Nascimento

Tanmay Nashte

Jorge Navarro

Pallavi Navnage

Priten Nayak

Joshua Neidish

Divya Nelluri

Paul Nelmes

Anshuman Nene

Kevin Neveu

Maria Newark

Charles Newark

William Newman

Ruby Ng Yi Ting

Wai Mun Ngan

Lambert Nguyen

Vincent Nguyen

Robert Nieman

Sushma Nivargi

Derek Nordaune

Ernest Nortey

Jeffery Novak

Venkata Nukala

Ramesh Nune

David Nuno Heredia

Leelaprasad Nuvvula

Uzor Nwachukwu

Carl Nyquist

Claas-Tido Ochtrop

Robert O'Connor

Chad O'Connor

Michael O'Grady

Gyanendra Ojha

Daisaku Okada

Judith Okafor

Hiroyuki Okuma

John Okunski

Thomas O'Leary

Patrick O'Loughlin

Aidan O'Neill

Kiat Beng Ong

Marquis Onorato

Anthony Ordak

Brian O'Rourke

Graydon Orr

Morgan Osder

Elizabeth Oseguera

Bruno Ostan

Sumit Oswal

Somnal Oth

Christopher Otten

Antoine Oudot De Dainville

Santosh Oza

Srikanth Pachala

Glenn Pacolay

Marc Padberg

Nidhi Padia

Nisha Pala

Andres Palacios

Snehal Palkar

Jose Alberto Palomares

Carmen Pan

Lei Pan

Divya Pandey

Pradipkumar Pandit

Karan Panesar

Praktan Pant

Prajakta Pant

Lauren Paolini

Niraj Parikh

Sam Park

Ben Parker

Marisela Parra

Ekta Parwani

Lakhan Pasari

Alexander Pasieka

Paul Pasker

Matthew Pasquini

Sourabh Pataskar

Parsh Patel

Bhautik Patel

Pritesh Patel

Abhishek Patel

Chintan Patel

Porus Patell

Phannga Pathammavong

Bismay Pati

Bhagyashree Patil

Jayesh Patil

Anurag Patsariya

Chandar Pattabhiram

Ravindranath Patyam

William Patzer

Paul Pavlish

Brian Pavlovich

Anagha Pawale

Ajay Pawar

Prajakta Pawar

William Pawson

Julian Peebles

Stephane Pelchat

Stefania Pendenza

Karen Pendlebury

Damian Pennell

Natalia Pereira

Gabriel Perez

Jeffrey Petersen

Fabien Petiau

Kevin Petrella

James Petrillo

Alexandre Pham

Gautam Phanse

Julian Philips

Janna Phillips

Joseph Piazza

Nitin Pillay

Prabodhi Pimplekar

Ann Marie Pinkerton

Karen Piry

Kelly Pitt

Nicolas Pittet

Richard Piva

Charlotte Plamondon

Clinton Pohler

Julie Polinsky

McKenna Pomidoro

Ganesh Veera Kumar Ponipireddy

Jeremie Ponseel

Clive Pope

Jonathan Porta Perez Martin

Siva reddy Pothireddy

Milind Powar

Brett Powell

Stephanie Power-Boehm
Vidya Poyilath
Ameet Prabhu Salgaonkar
Dipeshkumar Prajapati
Jitendra Prasad Nayak
Kara Prentice
Diego Prina
Andrew Prince
Edmund Pritchard
Virath Prithviraj
Julie Prochasson-Restrepo
Varshita Produtoor
Sylvain Prunier
Varun Prusty
Naga Aswani Puduru
Sathish Pulipati
John Purcell
Ashok Pusarla
Michael Qandah
Bianca Queiroz
Jean-Marc Quenet
Vence Michael Quirante
Faraz Qureshi
Bernard Rabjohns
Siavash Rad
Christopher Radding
Sivayoga Radha
Mathias Radtke
Charles Rafferty
Pankaj Rai
Sanyo Rai
Sanket Rajadhyaksha
Ramachandran Rajagopalan
Rasadurai Rajavaheinthan
Praveen Rajuri
Murarisetty Rakesh
Sreyashi Rakshit
Sivapriya Ramachandran
Rajiv Ramachandran
Somaram Ramakrishna Reddy
Anand Ramakrishnan
Arjun Ramaratnam

Amar Ramdhave
Nicolas Rametta
Tarun Reddy Ramidi
Amanda Ramsey
Pramod Rana
Smita Ranade
Zachary Randles
Luis Rangel das Neves
Guruprasad Rao
Sanjeev Rao
Chandra Rao
Thomas Rasmussen
Neelima Rathi
Kiran Ratnapu
Shivkumar Ravindran
Ravi Ravuri
Tushar Rawal
Marie Ray
Ajay Rayalwar
Harish Reddy Reddy
Sravanthi Reddyboina
Joseph Reed
Christopher Reed
Grant Reed
Mark Reed
Allison Reid
Gunter Remoy
Daphne Reurslag
Josue Reyes
Blake Rhymer
Anthony Rich
Sascha Richert
Andrew Rick
Pascal Rickenbacher
Kenneth Ricketts
Mark Riggs
Timothy Riley
Stephane Rinsoz
Leonardo Riviello
Richard Roberts
Joe Robertson
Anya Robertson

Helen Robson
Sydney Rodrigues
Jose Rodriguez
Kyle Rodriguez
Mary Roesch
Charles Rogers
Thomas Rohn
Chase Roles
Laura Roll
Nicole Romoli
Isaac Rosado
Karsten Rose
Matthew Rosenthal
Bradley Rosintoski
Dirk Rothe
Troy Rothert
Rob Rousou
John Rowley
Hollie Rowsell
Stuart Roy
Subhendu Roy
Thomas Ruane
Kevin Rucker
Sophia Ruiz
Ahmed Rukhsar
Mark Rushmere
Jesse Russell
Bruno Russo
Sandra Ryan
Carl Rydbeck
Ahmad Sadeddin
Nilendu Saha
Prosenjit Saha
Deepak Sahoo
Ashish Saihgal
Maryline Saladin
Kim Salkind
Sampo Salmi
Matthew Salud
Akshay Salunke
Nitin Salunke
Riyaz Samnani

David Sanders

Tom Sanders

Sukhmani Sandhu

Tejal Sanghvi

Wimonrat Sangthong

Lucas Santos

Sukrut Sarnobat

Satish Satalluri

Stephanie Satariano

Ajoy Satheesh

Joshua Sato

Megan Savage

Todd Savage

Michael Schanker

Matthew Schechtman

Joseph Schembri

Florian Scherrer

Joern Schlappinger

Christoff Schmalz

Paul Schroeder

Ines Schroeter

Alex Schwartzman

Joe Scott

Michael Scott

Manu Sebastian

Thomas Segeren

Omar Sehgal

Remigious Sekidde

Jake Sells

Jayakanthan Selvaraj

Aleksandrina Semova

Ramesh Sencha

Debanjan Sengupta

Vaishnavidevi Senthilraj

Breanna Sevy

Matthew Seyhun

Tatiana Shabanova

Tamir Shafer

Dhara Shah

Chirag Shah

Priyank Shah

Asokumar Shanmugam

Kaushal Sharma

Rimpi Sharma

Swati Sharma

Ayush Sharma

Aakanksha Sharma

Ankit Sharma

Neetal Sharma

Brian Shaw

Daniel Shchyokin

Abdul Sheik

Wendi Shen

Yongjing Shi

Mrunal Shinde

Aparajita Shinde

Akshay Shirole

Akash Shivhare

Arthur Shlendak

Grigoriy Shlyapinkov

James Shreckengost

Prateek Shrivastava

Nishithkumar Shukla

Pranav Shukla

AbdulLatif Siddiqui

Mohd Siddiqui

Tariq Siddiqui

Deborah Silberman

Manikanta Simma

James Simmons

Elizabeth Simpson

Bradley Simpson

Saskia Sinclair Donner

Mohana Singaluri

Atish Singh

Abhimanyu Singh

Rupali Singh

Gaurav Singh

Navjeet Singh

Jitendra Prakash Singh

Bhuwan Singla

Ankur Singla

Pierre-Andre Sinoir

Ali Sipahi

Ovidiu-Gheorghe Sipos

Narendra Singh Sisodiya

Brent Sisson

Jonathon Siudut

Joseph Skomurski

Sean Slattery

Fredrik Slettestøl

Richard Slipec

Brooke Smailes

Andy Smit

Shannah Smith

Erin Smith

Benjamin Smith

Michael Smith

Rebecca Smyth

Robert Snyder

Mark Sobota

Surabhi Solanke

Rubén Solla Medina

Raghunandan Somaraju

Deepthi Somasunder

Lars Sommer

Akshay Soni

Ketaki Sontakke

Ankita Sonune

Kyle Soroka

Visvanath Soundaranathan

Thomas Speich

Cecily Spikes

Laurent Spohr

Gerald Spoor

Suhas Sreedhar

Sunil Sridhar

Madhavi Sringarapu

Saimadhav Sriperumbudur

Amit Srivastava

Aakash Srivastava

Rachana Srivastava

Shailesh Srivastava

Sean Stacks

Robert Stambaugh

Daniella Stanghellini

Douglas Stapleton
Johan Stenfelt
Sally Stephens
Justin Stern
Yona Stern
Nicolas Stilleson
Richard Stone
Richard Stoney
Fitzhugh Stratton
Jason Strong
John Stroud
Jonathan Stueve
Paul Stuker
Patrick Sullivan
Jason Summers
Gexin Sun
Shanghua Sun
Thuwaragan Sundaramoorthy
Karl Sundequist Blomdahl
Prasad Surase
Bhanu Suri
Bhavya Surkanti
Mallikarjun Surukanti
Tommaso Susini
Craig Suyematsu
Michael Suzuki
Samata Swamy
James Sweeney
Derrick Sweet
Amer Uddin Syed
Ian Sykes
Virginia Synnott
Michelle Sztuk
Stefano Tagliabue
Sumakshi Talwar
Amit Tambe
Chetan Tamboli
Kuan Ju Tan
Shinsuke Tanaka
Gustaf Tanate
Kengsreng Tang
Priyanka Tapar

Michelle Tapping
Naim Tate
Gunjan Taunk
Dean Tayara
Peter Taylor
Philippa Taylor
Michelle Taylor
Steve Taylor Jr.
Andrew Tegan
Débora Teixeira
Kristien Templin
Troy Testerman
Tahsin Thakkar
Sonali Thakur
Mayuresh Thakur
Ravi Thakur
Bujji Babu Thangadancha
Rekha Thangellapalli
Rupak Thapa
Kalpana Spoorthy Thatipelly
Kieran Theron
Siyad Theyparambil
   Mohammed
Bharath Thippaiahgari
Austin Thompson
Robert Thoms
Grant Thorburn
Stacey Thornberry
Ravichandraprasad Thota
Vijayasree Thumuluri
Douglas Tilley
Anthony Tiscornia
Ruchi Tiwari
Shweta Tiwari
Richard Toalson
Vincent Toesca
Hunpin Toh
Michael Tommack
Julie Tonkin
Alex Torres
Adrianna Tozzi
Sven-Karsten Treskatis

Natasha Treskin
Nicholas Triantafel
Peter Trice
Helen Trim
Erin Triman
Tony Tripp
Peter Truman
Harrison Tsai
Eric Tsoi
Samantha Tsokris
Daniel Tunnicliffe
Srinivas Kartheek Turlapati
Robin Turner
Andrew Turner
Chris Turner
Apoorva Tyagi
Barbara Tygesen
Nadir Uddin
Rajashree Umbarkar
Pramod Upadhya
Saurabh Upadhyay
Amareshwari Uppara
David Uriarte
Ferdinand Uribe
Gabriel Uribe Mondragon
Iniobong Uto-Uko
Amit Utreja
Vaijayanti Vaidya
Ayushi Vaishnava
Swathi Vaitla
Dennis Vaje
Eric Valdes
Jose Valdivia Leon
Eshwar Valluripalli
Trishanth Vallurupalli
Jan van der Kooij
Matthew van Veenendaal
Surendranatha Vantla
Renukeswara Varikuti
Nitin Vatsya
Chance Vaughan
Devashri Vaychal

Jerry Vaz

Dharanidharan Vedantham

Sree Murali Krishna Veluvali

Sangeetha Venkatraman

Blanca Vera Mella

Patrice Verbeek

Dean Verhey

Carlos Viali

Vikas Vijayan

Amit Vijayant

Raul Villarreal Jr.

Reshma Vincent

Miguel Vives

Michelle Voller

Jutta von Ebbe

Matthew Waggett

Michael Wagner

Kyle Wagner

Farzad Wahab

Adinath Walke

Justin Walls

Kristine Walsh

Charlene Wang

Anil Wankhade

Raksha Wankhede

Aaron Wargo

Sophie Warwick

James Watson

Daniel Webiörn

David Webster

Matthew Weigand

Myles Weinstein

Michael Weir

Eric Weitz

Angela Welchel

Robert Wener

Jochen Werner

Travis Wheeler

Robert Whitcher

Adrianna White

Christopher White

Johnny White

Tracy White

Sophia White

Milissa White

Kaitlin Whitney

William Whitten

Axel Wiegand

Bobbie Wilcoxen

Donna Wilczek

Stephen Will

Jonathan Will

Lisa Williams

Philip Williams

Bettye Williams

Yasmir Williams

Andrew Williams

Craig Williams

David Williams

Craig Williams

Mattias Willman

John Willoughby

Gary Wilson

David Wilson

Clayton Wilson

Aaron Wilson

Simon Wilson

Robert Windesheim

Corine Winfield

Kjetil Winsnes

Matthew Wint

Steven Winter

Jamie Wodetzki

Timothy Wolfe

Joshua Wolfe

Michal Wolosz

David Wolstencroft

David Wondolowski

Khee Wong

Stephen Woo

Mark Woodbury

Brent Wooden

Elisa Woodward

Dana Wright

Peter Wu

Johan Wu

William Wyrick

Wenqian Xu

Andrew Xu

Murillo Yabiko

Jose Antonio Yabuki

Sunil Kumar Yalamanchili

Yukari Yamada

Vinay Yamsani

Michael Yan

Vijaya Krishna Yanamadala

Yao Yao

Sherman Yap

Samata Yarlagadda

Ali Yawar

Spandana Yellannagari

Raja Sekhar Yerram

Fredrik Ygge

Lori Yonelunas

Douglas Young

Neil Young

Hongyang Yu

Scott Yu

Troy Zachary

Michael Zaczek

Christoph Zahn

Amber Zamlich

Samuel Zbinden

Bradley Zediker

Tulsi Zeidman

Wei Zhang

Lei Zhao

Yingbo Zhao

Ryan Zhou

Katherine Zilm

John Zimmerman

Robyn Zimmermann

Jacob Zuiderent

INDEX

Note: Page numbers followed by an italicized *n* indicate a note.

ABOUT COUPA

Coupa's Business Spend Management (BSM) platform empowers finance and procurement leaders to spend *smarter, simpler,* and *safer.* With more than $2 trillion of transactional spend under management across its global customer base, Coupa offers businesses—from the Fortune 1000 to the world's fastest-growing organizations—the visibility and control needed to manage costs, mitigate risks, and scale for growth in one comprehensive and open platform in the cloud. For more information, visit www.coupa.com.

ABOUT COMMUNITY INTELLIGENCE

Coupa Community Intelligence is an analytics engine powered by artificial intelligence (AI) that "listens" objectively to trillions of dollars of transactional spend data flowing through the Coupa Business Spend Management Platform and prescribes instant insights that help companies spend *smarter, simpler,* and *safer.* Built in the cloud, Coupa has unique access to transactional business data, which enables its Community Intelligence engine to leverage the latest in machine learning and AI to provide accurate benchmarks and unprecedented high-value insights.

ABOUT ROB

Rob Bernshteyn is the chairman of the board and chief executive officer at Coupa, where he oversees the company's strategy and execution. Under his leadership over the past decade, Coupa has grown from a small start-up company to a multi-billion-dollar public organization driving measurable value for enterprises around the world. Rob is an accomplished executive with over two decades of experience in the enterprise software industry. He holds a BS in Management Information Systems from the State University of New York at Albany and an MBA from Harvard Business School.